PENGUIN VEER

# THE EXTRAORDINARY LIFE OF RIFLEMAN AURANGZEB

A storyteller at heart, Damini Punia specializes in military narratives, particularly those rooted in the Kashmir Valley—a region that resonates deeply with her soul. She is the co-author of *Operation Khukri: The True Story Behind the Indian Army's Most Successful Mission as Part of the United Nations* (2021). Educated at Lady Shri Ram College, Delhi, Damini's sharp intellect complements her passion for uncovering the complexities of human experience, allowing her to delve into the untold stories that shape our world.

An adventure enthusiast and animal lover, Damini is guided by a strong belief in the power of karma and strives to lead a life of kindness and compassion. She believes that if her words can inspire and enlighten future generations, her purpose in this world will be fulfilled.

# THE EXTRAORDINARY LIFE OF
# RIFLEMAN AURANGZEB

## DAMINI PUNIA

**PENGUIN**
**VEER**

An imprint of Penguin Random House

PENGUIN VEER

Penguin Veer is an imprint of the Penguin Random House group of companies
whose addresses can be found at global.penguinrandomhouse.com

Published by Penguin Random House India Pvt. Ltd
4th Floor, Capital Tower 1, MG Road,
Gurugram 122 002, Haryana, India

Penguin
Random House
India

First published in Penguin Veer by Penguin Random House India 2025

10 9 8 7 6 5 4 3 2

ISBN 9780143464099

Typeset in Adobe Garamond Pro by MAP Systems, Bengaluru, India
Printed at Gopsons Papers Pvt. Ltd., Noida

www.penguin.co.in

100%
Paper from well-
managed forests
FSC® C191020

*To my parents . . . thank you*

*2025: The year of miracles*

औरंगजेब मेरे बेटे,

आज बरसों बाद, दिल में जो दर्द है, उसे अल्फाजों में बयां करने की कोशिश कर रहा हूँ। मेरे बेटे, तुम्हारे बगैर हमारा घर सूना है। तुम्हारी अम्मी हर रोज उसी राह को तकती रहती हैं, जैसे तुम लौट आओगे। वो घंटों इन्तजार करती हैं, मगर तुम वापस नहीं आओगे, ये हकीकत हमें हर रोज सताती है।

तुम्हारे बिना हमने २०१८ के बाद से कभी भी ईद की खुशियां नहीं मनाईं। हर साल, जब ईद आती है, राज बेगम की आँखों में वही गम और खालीपन होता है, जैसे कोई चीज़ छीन ली गई हो। तुमसे मुलाकात का रुझान तो कभी खत्म नहीं हुआ, और तुम्हारी अम्मी हर बार उसी उम्मीद में बैठ जाती है, जैसे कोई चमत्कार हो और तुम लौट आओ। हम जानते हैं कि तुम अब हमारे दरमियान नहीं हो मगर इस सच्चाई को कबूल करना बेहद मुश्किल है।

बेटा तुमने हमेशा अपनी जिम्मेदारी निभाई, हमेशा मुल्क के लिए कुछ बड़ा करने की बात की। बेटा मैं और तुम्हारी अम्मी तुम पर बेहद फख्र महसूस करते हैं। लेकिन अब यह फख्र भी कहीं खो सा गया है। तुम्हारे बगैर हम सब अधूरे हैं। तुम्हारे भाई-बहन, तुम्हारी अम्मी और मैं तुमसे बेहद मोहब्बत करते हैं।

मैं और राज बेगम, हर दिन तुम्हारी यादों में जीते हैं। हम तुम्हारी मुस्कुराहट, तुम्हारी आवाज़ फिर से सुनने के लिए बेचैन रहते हैं। तुम से हर बात कह सकता हूँ। मेरे बेटे - तुम हमेशा हमारे दिलों में जिंदा रहोगे, चाहे तुम पास हो या ना हो। हमें गर्व है हमने एक वीर पुत्र को जन्म दिया। तुम हमेशा हमारे लिए जिंदा रहोगे।

हमेशा तुम्हारी यादों में,
तुम्हारे अब्बू
मोहम्मद हनीफ

Aurangzeb, my beloved son,

After many years, I am trying to put the pain in my heart into words. My son, our home is empty without you. Every day, your mother gazes down the same path, hoping you'll return. She waits for hours, but the truth that you won't come back haunts us every single day.

Since 2018, we haven't celebrated Eid with any joy. Every year, as Eid approaches, Raj Begum's eyes reflect the same sorrow and emptiness, as though something precious has been taken from her. The dream of seeing you again never fades, and your mother always sits, hoping for a miracle that will bring you back. But deep down, we know you're no longer with us, and accepting this painful reality is almost impossible.

Son, you always took your responsibilities seriously and always spoke of doing something meaningful for the country. Both your mother and I are immensely proud of you. But now, every day, that pride feels diminished because, without you, we are incomplete. Your siblings, your mother and I—we all love you endlessly, and every single day, we remember you.

The sacrifice you made will forever be etched in our hearts. We understand you did your duty, but the cost we have paid for that is something no one else can truly understand.

Raj Begum and I live each day with your memories. Your joy, your laughter, your words—they are forever with us. Your smile, your voice—they will never leave our hearts. I can say only one thing to you, my son: you will always be alive in our hearts, whether or not you are with us physically.

We are so proud of what you did, but the yearning to see you again will never go away. You will remain in our hearts forever, my son.

Always in your memories,

Your father,
Mohammad Hanief

# Contents

# Introduction

Sometimes, life has a way of guiding you to the stories you're meant to tell. I never imagined that a trip to Kashmir would lead me to a moment that would change everything. It was a room full of people, talking, laughing and sharing their lives. But in the corner, there was Raj Begum. While there physically, her heart and soul seemed to be somewhere else. Her eyes, distant and lost in thought, spoke of something deeper—a quiet ache that only those who have lost something or someone could truly understand. The profound, unspoken grief amid the silence was like a whisper in my ear, telling me: *This is the story you need to write.*

It was Raj Begum, in all her stillness, who confirmed what I already knew—this book would be about sacrifice, unfulfilled love and dreams, a festival that would never be celebrated and a legacy that would remain untold. And at the heart of it all, stood Rifleman Aurangzeb.

Let me tell you—this wasn't an easy path. Writing this book felt like climbing a mountain with no end in sight. There were days when I thought I'd never find the right words to do justice to a man as remarkable as Aurangzeb, long nights spent staring at a blank screen, wondering how I could capture the essence of his courage, sacrifice and the unfulfilled love that defined his life. I would start and stop, start and stop. The pressure of doing justice to his story, family and legacy made me feel like I was carrying a heavy burden, one that I, at times, wasn't sure I could bear. But then, in the midst of my frustration, I would think of Aurangzeb. I would think of his resilience in the face of impossible odds. I would think of how, despite everything he endured, he never faltered. And with that thought, I would sit up straight and push forward, just like he did.

There was one moment during my research that broke through the difficulty and reminded me why I was doing this. When I visited Raj Begum's home, she welcomed me like family. And, in one of the most beautiful acts of hospitality I've ever experienced, she fed me Aurangzeb's favourite food—makki ki roti with ghee and shakkar. I kid you not, the moment that warm, golden roti touched my plate, something changed. I was connecting with Aurangzeb in a way I had never anticipated. I could almost see him sitting at the table, enjoying the simple comfort of that meal, and suddenly I understood a little more about him—not just as a soldier but as a human. Slowly, I started to understand that this book was not just about a soldier's bravery or the heroic battles he fought. It was about his promise to his soulmate— a promise that would never be fulfilled. A love that was pure and unbroken, even in death. It is this love, this unspoken connection between him and the woman he had promised to return to, that became the thread weaving through the heart of the book.

But the person who truly helped me push through this journey was my mother. She never asked me how the book was going, but I could always tell when she was thinking about it. She would walk around the house, pointing to walls as though the framed cover of my book was already hanging there. 'This is where it will go,' she'd say, always with that quiet faith in me, even when I doubted myself. Her belief in this book, in *me*, was the anchor I needed. Every time I felt lost, I'd think of her faith and keep going. Without her, this book would never have seen the light of day. It's her love, constant belief and quiet strength that I owe so much to.

As I sit here now, looking back on the months I spent bringing this story to life, I realize that writing about Aurangzeb was not just an act of research or storytelling—it was a way of paying tribute to a man whose life was marked by sacrifice, love and an unshakable commitment to something greater than himself. It was about honouring a soldier who gave his everything for each of us.

Aurangzeb's story is a reminder that there are so many like him—men and women who sacrifice without expectation of recognition. They are the ones who ensure that we can sleep peacefully at night, yet their stories often go untold. This book, for me, is a tribute—not just to Aurangzeb but to all the soldiers who fought and continue to fight for our safety. I hope that by sharing his story, I can inspire future generations to remember the sacrifices made for our freedom. I want my readers to understand that heroes come in all forms—even if they're not the ones who make it to the headlines sometimes, they are the ones who leave an indelible mark on our hearts.

And as I sit here, reflecting on everything that led me to this point, I realize that this book is not just mine. It's all of ours. It's the story of a man who gave everything, and a story of a mother who will never forget the son she lost. It's a reminder that in the smallest of moments, we find the strength to carry on. This is not just Aurangzeb's story; it's our story too. And I hope that in telling it, we can honour all those who've given so much, and ensure their stories live on, long after we're gone.

So, here it is—my tribute to Rifleman Aurangzeb, a man whose courage and love will never fade. And who knows? Maybe, just maybe, the next time you sit down to enjoy a warm meal, you'll think of him too.

And so, with a heart full of gratitude to Raj Begum, to my mother and to the spirit of Aurangzeb, I present this book to you. I hope, as you read these pages, you will remember that even in the darkest times, love remains. Even when a promise cannot be fulfilled, it endures.

This is his story. This is *our* story. And I hope that, in telling it, we can keep his spirit alive for generations to come.

# #1

# The Stubborn Child

**Salani, Poonch**
**5 February 1994**

It was a tense and unsettling scene. A man in a military uniform with his face obscured, being dragged by figures with hidden faces. The soldier appeared tall and robust, dressed in olive green camouflage, struggling against tight ropes, barely conscious amidst the relentless torment. Suddenly, the situation took a harrowing turn. Without warning, the air erupted in a storm of gunfire. Bullets rained down mercilessly upon the soldier, each shot cutting through the air with a chilling precision.

With the piercing sound of the gunshot, Raj Begum woke up breathless and overwhelmed with fear, her body trembling and drenched in sweat. As a pregnant woman in her ninth month, the experience was deeply unsettling—a nightmare had gripped her heart in terror. The horrific dream left Raj Begum reeling with questions and anguish. Who was the man in uniform? Was it her husband, Mohammad

Hanief, stationed along the Line of Actual Control? The uncertainty gnawed at her, twisting her thoughts into a whirlwind of distress. With no means to contact Hanief and a mind plagued by a troubled vision, Raj Begum felt utterly inconsolable. As if the nightmare wasn't distressing enough, her anxiety heightened when she felt her contractions start. Each wave of pain reminded her sharply of her vulnerability and intensified her need for reassurance. In the middle of the tornado of emotions, Raj Begum searched desperately for comfort. Her heart weighed heavily with the ominous dream that seemed to foretell something inauspicious.

* * *

The cold wind had engulfed Salani. It had snowed pretty heavily the previous night and the village rooftops were adorned with a quilt of freshly fallen snow, where each flake was like a masterpiece painted from the brush of winter. There, in the crisp air, one could hear the soft moans of Raj Begum. The men had gathered outside Hanief's residence, huddled under a khubani[1] tree with a kangri[2] in the middle. The children of the village were swirling through the row of trees around the house. Raj Begum was writhing in pain, lying on a woven wooden bed. The expectant mother was surrounded by a circle of women who had gathered to lend their support. She laboured with the strength and resilience of generations before her in a small, dimly lit room adorned

---

[1] Apricot tree.

[2] An earthen pot woven around with wicker filled with hot embers used by people in Kashmir to keep the chill at bay.

with handwoven tapestries and dried herbs. Her soft moans were met with soothing words and comforting touches from the women who stood by her side, their faces etched with empathy and love. They had been through this ritual of birth many times; their collective wisdom was passed down through generations.

As the sun shifted west, the sky became a canvas painted with pink, lavender and indigo hues. Stars emerged gradually like diamond dust sprinkled across the heavens. The stillness was profound and, soon enough, the most beautiful sound in the world—the cry of a newborn echoed through the valley of Salani. However, this cry was different; it wasn't the usual quivering note of a baby but more like a battle cry against the unknown. It was a cry that held the promise of a lifetime, a story waiting to be written, an adventure yet to unfold. As the cry reverberated through the room, it touched the hearts of all present. Tears welled up in the eyes of Raj Begum, who marvelled at the miracle of this new life. The moon bore testimony to the birth of a future star. Beautiful amber eyes looked around as if claiming his position in the world. Raj Begum was tired yet ecstatic as her eyes met her firstborn Shabieen and son Qasim, who were curiously peeping through the brown curtains.

When she called out to them, they entered the room bewildered to see this tiny creation of God resting next to his mother. Qasim jumped on the bed from one side and touched his younger brother's cheek with a trembling finger; the first brush made him smile from ear to ear. His eyes, wide with wonder, transported him to another world where the initial thought that crossed his mind was—'Now, I have a partner in crime, and I can't wait to flaunt my brother to Afzal and the other boys.' The Muezzin's evening call to prayer jolted Qasim back to his senses. Unable to control his excitement, Qasim kissed the back of his mother's hand and ran outside to share the joyous tidings with his companions.

Raj Begum's face had a symphony of emotions expressing happiness, yet her eyes spoke otherwise. She missed the man of her life—the intertwining of hands and the romantic whispers—as their family increased by one. While Salani was celebrating the miracle of birth, Hanief, sitting in his camouflage at 10,000 ft amidst the thick foliage of Arunachal Pradesh, was utterly unaware of the birth of his son. Raj Begum's last letter to Hanief expressed her longing for him, his mother's health condition and how they could be parents any day now. Hanief would sit on the banks of the Namka Chu River with the letter close to his chest, dreaming about Raj Begum. The emerald-green dupatta draped on her head, with a strand of her locks weaving an intricate dance on her face, was the image Hanief carefully carried in his heart when he left for duty after his last leave. With tearful eyes carrying unspoken feelings, Raj Begum embraced her newborn in her arms. His almond-shaped amber eyes were fixated on Raj Begum, and his curly locks were evidence of his relationship with his mother.

Aurangzeb had been an attention-seeking baby since he was born; and rightly so, he was the centre of everybody's universe. Six months after his birth, Hanief came home on leave to be pleasantly surprised by the news of becoming a father to a newborn son. The letter that Raj Begum wrote divulging the news of the birth had gotten misplaced in transit. Hanief got off at the bus stop at Meander, a small town near his native village, Salani. He met Gaffar Miya, who used to work at the masjid in town and was from Salani as well. Upon seeing Hanief from the masjid window, he called out to him, rushed down the wooden spiral stairway and hugged him. '*Bhai Jaan, iss baar itna samay kahan laga diya?*' (Brother, what took you so long?), Gaffar Miya enquired. Hanief's instant reply was, '*Bas fauj ki naukri hai, desh sewa ka koi samay nahi hota*' (I am in the Indian Army, and service of the nation is not time-bound). Gaffar Miya instantly kicked off his motorbike and asked Hanief to hop on. Through the winding roads, Hanief's expectant eyes were waiting for one glimpse of Raj Begum since it had been over 180 days since they had seen each other. He was longing to hear her oh-so-melodious voice say, *As-Salaam Alaikum*. As soon as Gaffar Miya stopped the vehicle, Hanief jumped up and ran through the village road. '*Arey Hanief, tumhara bag reh gaya*' (Hanief, you left your bag here), Gaffar Miya screamed, but it did not affect Hanief's pace. He rushed to the field next to their thatched hut to find Raj Begum harvesting the crop, tip-toed from behind and grabbed Raj Begum by the waist. Taken aback, she immediately turned around to hit the 'stranger' with an axe. Had Hanief not stopped his Begum, the surprise would have been deadly. When Raj Begum's eyes met Hanief, she couldn't believe what she saw. '*Arey kya hua Begum? Aa gaya main*' (What happened to you, Begum? I'm here now), Hanief exclaimed. Upon hearing him call her name, Raj Begum knelt on the ground and broke into tears. Hanief immediately got down to his knees and hugged his lifeline to be able to breathe again. That embrace felt like an eternity; it was as though, at that moment, time stood still. Holding hands, the two of them walked their way home. Raj Begum was excited for Hanief to meet the new member. '*Pata hai kab se raah dekh raha hai Jevi?'* (You know, Jevi has been waiting for you since long), Raj Begum said. *'Jevi? Yeh naam kisne rakha?'* (Jevi? Who decided on the name?), Hanief enquired. *'Maulvi*[3] *ji Aqeeqah*[4] *adaa karne aaye the. Unhone kaha ki iska naam Jevi rakho kyunki yeh hamesha amar rahega'* (Maulvi ji visited to perform Aqeeqah and told me to name him Jevi as he would live forever), Raj Begum explained. Hanief smiled. Upon reaching home, he entered the room to find little Jevi away with the fairies. He softly embraced his cute button hands and kissed the back of his palm. Tears rolled down Hanief's face as he stood still, thinking of all the moments he had missed with Jevi. *'Abu! Abu!'* (Father! Father!), Qasim came running and sprang to Hanief's arms. Hanief embraced Qasim close to his chest while Raj Begum got nun chai[5] for him in a brass samovar.[6] Hanief sat in front of the ancient hearth on their verandah and enjoyed the chai with his Begum; a moment that he had been waiting for forever. As the sun shifted west, the couple enjoyed each other's company and tried to compensate for all the days they were away.

Hanief's time in Salani flew like the wind, and it was soon time for him to leave. On his last day home, Hanief woke up rather gloomy. *'Kya hua? Tabiyat theek hai?'* (What happened? I hope you're feeling okay?), Raj Begum enquired. Hanief didn't have an answer. He silently wished for time to

---

[3] Muslim religious scholar or cleric.

[4] Aqeeqah refers to the sacrifice that is offered on behalf of the newborn on the seventh day after birth.

[5] Also known as Kashmiri tea or pink tea made with green tea leaves, milk and baking soda.

[6] A brass tea urn used in Jammu and Kashmir.

stay still and absorb most of the moment. As was his ritual for the last day, Hanief dressed in a crisp black Pathani suit[7] with *sozni*[8] embroidery on the collar and went to the village *mazar*[9] to pray for his family's health.

On his way home, he came across three men sitting encircling a kangri. '*Aur, Hanief Miya, desh bhakti ho gayi ho toh aaiye hum bhi haath milaein*' (Hanief brother, if you are done with your patriotic dreams, let's join hands). '*Aslam, desh bhakti koi kaam nahi hai, jeene ka tarika hai mere liye. Jitna jaldi tum bhi sahi raah pe aa jaoge, tumhare liye behtar hoga*' (Aslam, patriotism is not a chore for me but a way of life, and the sooner you understand this fact, the better it will be for you), Hanief retorted. Aslam and a few young boys from Salani had gotten brainwashed by the radio messages from across the border, polarizing the youth on religious lines—so much so that he started working as a guide for the infiltrators and helped them settle in safe houses in and around Salani. Hanief didn't halt a minute longer around them and left for home immediately as he didn't want to miss even a minute of these last few hours with Raj Begum, God alone knew when they would be reunited. On the way, he plucked some white flowers and wrapped them in a garland for his Begum. He had always been big on the gestural expression of love and enjoyed making his woman feel special whenever he was around.

'*Raj Begum, kidhar ho? Raj Begum?*' (Raj Begum, where are you? Raj Begum?), Hanief started shouting while looking

---

[7] An ethnic outfit for men comprising a kurta and salwar.

[8] A popular needlepoint embroidery technique from the Kashmir valley.

[9] A mausoleum or shrine in some places of the world, typically that of a saint or notable religious leader.

for her everywhere. Raj Begum was roasting the corn kernels on the *chulha*.[10] *'Kyun shor kar rahe hain janab?'* (Why are you making so much noise?) Raj Begum enquired with a spatula in one hand. The sun-yellow dupatta that adorned her head and the sunlight reflecting from it cast a spectacular glow on her face; Hanief was consumed. *'Aapse keh rahi hun main Qasim ke abbu, sun nahi raha?'* (Qasim's father, I am asking you, am I not audible?), Raj Begum asked again while swirling the dancing kernels on the pan. *'Kal se koi shor nahi karega, dekhiye kya laaye hain aapke liye'* (Nobody will make any noise after today. See what I got for you), Hanief replied while pulling the garland from his kurta's pocket. Hanief's gestures meant more to Raj Begum than even the prized Kohinoor. When he sat next to her and wrapped the garland on her wrist, almost instantly, she melted like an ice cream on a hot summer afternoon. Raj Begum's blushed cheeks showed what Hanief meant to her. She affectionately looked at Hanief while he relished the freshly roasted kernels. *'Apne gaon ki baat he kuch aur hai. Badi yaad aati hai unit jaane ke baad'* (There is something unique about our village. I miss it a lot while I am away), Hanief remarked with a mouth full of corn. *'Gaon ki yaad aati hai ya kisi shaks ki?'* (You miss the village or a particular person?), Raj Begum instantly enquired. Hanief could read between the lines and to tease her, he smirked, *'Haan, ammi*[11] *ki, Qasim ki, ab Jevi ki bhi, aur Maulvi sahab, aur bus adde pe chaiwala Bakhtiyar, kaafi lambi list hai'* (Yes, like my mother, Qasim, now Jevi as well, Maulvi sahab and also the tea-stall guy at the bus stand, Bakhtiyar; the list is long). While he was trying really hard to

---

[10] A traditional cooking stove made from clay, mud and cow dung.

[11] Mother in Urdu.

hold back his laughter, Raj Begum's face turned from a pleasant peach blush to raging red in a matter of seconds. '*Jaiye phir Bakhtiyar ko he boliye aapko bhutta sek ke dega*' (Go then, ask Bakhtiyar only to roast the corn kernels for you), Raj Begum retorted while taking away the bowl from Hanief's hand. '*Arey, aap toh naaraz ho gaye. Yaad usse kiya jata hai jo dur ho, aap toh humare dil mein ghar basaye baithi hain*' (You got angry. We miss those who are away; You have pitched your tent in my heart). Hanief held Raj Begum's hand. '*Mazaak apni jagah, gaon ka maahol kaafi bigad raha hai, aaj Aslam bhi mila masjid ke pass, aap apna aur ghar walon ka dhyan rakhiyega aur kuch bhi ho, pados mein Wajid miya ko awaaz lagaiyega. Baaki, aap fauji ki begum hai, khud poori fauj se kam thodi hain*' (Jokes apart, the environment in the village is getting pretty grim by the day. I met Aslam today outside the masjid. You, please look after yourself and everyone at home. If you sense anything shady, please call out to Brother Wajid, who lives next door, immediately. Rest, you're a soldier's wife and no less than an Army yourself), Hanief expressed. Though he was trying to motivate his wife, his heart lost a beat at the thought of leaving at the break of dawn the following day.

As the sun was trying to peek through, Hanief stood with his rucksack strapped to his back. Teary-eyed, Raj Begum, with the Quran in her hand, looked at him. Hanief kissed his boys goodbye and hugged Raj Begum. With his hands wrapped around her, the world came to a halt, and in that embrace, he wanted to take away all her misery and sadness. Hanief was finding it increasingly difficult to hold back his tears, so he decided to leave before he got too weak in his knees to even step out. Hanief crossed from under the Quran, which Raj Begum was holding, while she prayed for his safety. Such is the beauty of love, where two people silently pray for each other's happiness and wish to take away the sadness of one another. After Hanief left, Raj Begum receded to her room and offered *namaz*[12], praying for her husband's long life. Hanief traversed through the maize field, where each step he took away from his beloved made it feel like he was walking with weights tied to his ankle. Quite mechanically, he boarded the bus, and as the wind hit his face from the window, tears started rolling down as if his world had crashed. Hanief had always wanted to join the forces and serve his nation, but the only downside was being away from his beloved and not being there to hear her call him or whisper sweet nothings to her. His evening nun chai session with Raj Begum would get replaced by a quick cup of tea with his company buddies at a far-off post with nothing but memories to keep him sane. While sipping tea at some outpost, Hanief would often close his eyes to feel Raj Begum's presence around him. It was only after months that he would reach a point where, even after having his eyes closed, he would not be able to picture his wife, which would cause cyclones in his heart. Hanief's coping mechanism was to pour his heart out in ink and wait for the arrival of the unit postal person bringing all the letters from the base camp. Almost every day, Hanief would hope for his name to be called. '*Sipahi Hanief, aapke ghar se chitthi aayi hai*' (Sepoy Hanief, there is a letter for you)—a few words that, even though were loud, were more peaceful to him than the sound of *Azaan*.[13]

\* \* \*

---

[12] Islamic practice of prayer or worship.

[13] The Islamic call to prayer that is proclaimed five times a day, usually from the minaret of a mosque.

After months of separation, letters written with love and tears, and the family expanding every few years, Hanief retired from the forces in 1998. The two souls were now reunited as one, and Hanief wanted to compensate for the years he was away. '*Uth jao nalayakon,* school *nahi jana? Koi bolega fauji ki aulaad ho?*' (Wake up, my good-for-nothing kids. Don't you have to go to school? Who's going to say that you are a soldier's children?), Hanief would start every morning with this rousing reveille. Qasim, Aurangzeb, Tariq, Shabbir, Zafar and Shehnaaz would wake up in a domino effect and sit next to each other, huddled in a warm tosh blanket, and wait for their morning chai with the aroma of saffron that would wrap the once plain room into a blanket of warmth and sensory goodness. Sipping the golden nectar overlooking the snowclad mountains, all the children would be busy strategizing ways and means to use the bathing space before others to have a nice and dry place to themselves. At the same time, Hanief would help Raj Begum make makki ki roti[14] on the traditional mud chulha, transforming the mundane act of roti-making into a symphony of love and togetherness. Hanief, with battle-hardened hands, sitting next to his love, would knead the dough with a rhythmic grace while his wife would roll the dough to make the bread. As soon as the rolled dough met the hot surface of the cast iron skillet, a sizzling serenade would commence. Around the ancient hearth, Hanief would steal glances at his beautiful wife, and their shared laughter would echo off the earthy walls while the bread would rise and turn golden brown. In that intimate space, the couple would transcend the scars of their past

---

[14] A flat unleavened bread made from corn meal (maize flour).

separation. The soldier, now a taciturn bard of domesticity, revelled in the serenity of the kitchen—a refuge where love is kneaded into every fold of the dough and the echoes of war dissipate into the warmth of a shared homecoming. While the children would get dressed for school one after the other, Hanief would set up plates for his little warriors. He would generally eat his meals with his wife after all the children had eaten because he would never want his children to feel that their father didn't value them enough or to make his wife feel unloved.

## February 2002

While the first month of the year wrapped up, Salani delicately meandered towards spring. It was soon Aurangzeb's eighth birthday, and like every other year, he would make sure to remind everyone of 5 Feb like a broken record. '*Abu, Meander chalein?*' (Father, shall we go to Meander?), Aurangzeb implored. '*Abhi do din pehle he toh ration laye hain. Ab Meander mein kya hai?*' (We bought groceries just two days ago. What's there in Meander now?), Hanief questioned Aurangzeb while feeding the cows. Considering the stubborn kid that Aurangzeb was and the love his ammi had towards him, it was no surprise that in less time than it takes to blink, both Hanief and Aurangzeb were on the next bus to Meander. Standing at the market junction, Hanief, with a puzzled gaze, enquired about the direction of their move. Aurangzeb pointed towards the narrow alley next to the masjid wall. There, nestled in the labyrinth of the confined lane, was a narrow vintage shop with a sign board that read: 'Abdullah Feathers.' He was puzzled as to what Jevi could want from that shop. As excited as a kid in an amusement park, Aurangzeb rushed right through the emerald-carved half-open door. The tiny shop looked like it had been transported from ages ago. The rustic bell at the entrance, vintage pictures of different breeds of pigeons from across the world haphazardly hung on the butter-yellow walls, and a dust-covered table with chinar leaves carved placed on the left of the entrance all gave a glimpse into the world of a bygone era. Behind the carved table sat Abdullah miya, wrapped in the gentle folds of a charcoal grey Pathani suit, with each thread whispering the tales of distant lands and ancient times. Atop his silvered head sat the Muslim *topi*,[15] a crown of tradition that weaves together the threads of faith and culture. The edges of the topi, softened by time, lent an air of gentleness to the face beneath. Behind a pair of spectacles, his eyes, weathered by a lifetime of experiences, glinted with quiet resilience and a depth of understanding that only the passage of years could bestow. Just then, the curtain door swayed and a girl with a bounce in her step entered, filling the air with laughter. The embroidered pastel curtain gently settled back in place. '*Dada! Dada!*', The little girl in the pink dress came running with a natural skip in her step; an effortless rhythm that mirrored the excitement bubbling within her. 'Hanief miya, *inse miliye, humari poti Ilham*' (Hanief, meet her, my granddaughter, Ilham). Her dark, almond button eyes sparkled amidst the midnight strands on her face as she looked up and said, '*As-Salaam Alaikum!*' in her oh-so-sweet voice. At that moment, time stood still for Aurangzeb and the world around him blurred, and all that remained was the resonance of her voice.

---

[15] A hat.

Aurangzeb could not help but be glued to Ilham. '*Jevi, kya kaam hai? Jevi? Arey kya lene aaye ho?*' (Jevi, what do you want? Jevi? What do you want to buy?), Hanief kept enquiring, but Aurangzeb was lost in thought. It was only after Hanief nudged him that Aurangzeb blurted, '*do Ilham kabootar chahiye*' (I need two Ilham Pigeons). He couldn't believe the words that came out of his mouth. 'What a foolish guy', he thought to himself. '*Nahi nahi, mera matlab uss din ek pinjare mein do safed kabootar dekhe the voh chahiye*' (No, No, I mean I saw two white pigeons the other day in the cage; I want them), Aurangzeb corrected himself almost instantly.

'*Kabootar? Kabootar ka kya karoge tum? Tum logo ko paal rahe hai utna kaafi nahi hai ki yeh kabootar bhi paalne hain?*' (Pigeons? What will you do with the pigeons? Isn't that enough that we are raising all of you that you now want us to even have pigeons to worry about?), Hanief raised his eyebrows. '*Abbu, mera janamdin aa rha hai aur mujhe is saal yehi do kabutar chahiye. Vada karta hun ki iske alawa aur kuch nahi mangunga*' (Father, my birthday is approaching and I want these pigeons as a present. I promise I won't ask for anything else). Aurangzeb made a face that was hard to say no to. '*Theek hai, Abdullah miya, bataiye kitne ke hain kabootar?*' (Okay, Brother Abdullah, please tell me, how much are these pigeons for?) Hanief took out his wallet. '*Hanief bhai 2000 ka joda hai*' (Hanief brother, they are Rs 2000 a pair), Abdullah replied immediately. '*2000? Kabootar kharid rahe hain sona nahi*' (2000? We're buying pigeons, not gold). Hanief looked astonished. '*Hanief bhai janta hoon par yeh kabootar Kashmir ke nahi hain, bahar desh se mangwaye hain. Aapke bete ki aankhein kamaal hain, asli hira pehchaan leti hain*' (Brother Hanief, these pigeons are not from Kashmir. They have been imported. Your son has a good eye, these are rare gems), Abdullah replied. Hanief looked at Aurangzeb, as though silently urging him to reconsider. However, his son remained unfazed. His mind was fixed on the pigeons and his eyes on Ilham. After a few rounds of discussions, Hanief reluctantly gave in to Aurangzeb's erratic demands, and Aurangzeb happily left the store with the pigeons.

Hanief kept wondering, when children needed toys and clothes at this age, what would his son do with the pigeons? Aurangzeb travelled from Meander to Salani with his two friends on his lap. Upon reaching Salani, he flew like the wind to get home and introduced his new friends to his Ammi and siblings. They happily went to the garden with the pigeons. Hanief was puzzled, trying to understand Aurangzeb's thoughts. However, when Raj Begum asked Aurangzeb what he would do with the two pigeons, Hanief replied that he wanted to buy them as presents for his upcoming birthday. But before they could finish the conversation, Aurangzeb opened the cage and set the pigeons free. He was so happy that he laughed as if he had discovered a treasure. Hanief screamed, '*2000 rupaiye uda diye tumne ek he second mein*' (You wasted two thousand rupees in an instant). A few days ago, when Aurangzeb had gone to Meander to buy groceries with his dad, he had seen these pigeons outside the store, caged and looking sad. It was as if they were calling out to him while trying to escape from the cage. Aurangzeb couldn't shake off their memory from his mind and decided to buy their freedom as his present. Hanief was perplexed; while he didn't understand Aurangzeb's theories, Raj Begum was immensely proud of her son's considerate and humane qualities.

Apart from advocating for the voiceless, Aurangzeb had a daily routine he enjoyed. He loved having doodh and makhan.[16] However, he couldn't handle spicy food at all. On 5 February, as usual, Aurangzeb wore the new and crisp Pathani suit that his father had lovingly stitched. He then accompanied his father to the masjid to offer prayers. Afterwards, Aurangzeb returned home to a delicious spread of makke ki roti,[17] desi makhan and organic jaggery powder. As he was enjoying his birthday meal, Hanief played a prank on Aurangzeb by secretly placing a piece of spicy chilli pickle on his plate. Aurangzeb, of course, ate it and immediately felt the burning sensation, making him desperately reach for water. Raj Begum, always supportive of her son, sided with him and did not let Hanief get away with the prank. The incident became a light-hearted tale among family and friends, serving as a reminder of Aurangzeb's aversion to spicy food and his family's loving camaraderie.

Aurangzeb had always been a spirited and headstrong child with a penchant for grandeur in everything he did—be it his choice of attire, his preferences in food or his aspirations for the future. One particular incident from his childhood, often retold with amusement by his father, Mohammad Hanief, paints a vivid picture of Aurangzeb's stubbornness and flair for drama.

It was sometime around the harvest season when the fields were alive with the fresh scent of ripe maize. Hanief and his wife were toiling diligently under the warm sun, gathering the crops they had nurtured with care. Meanwhile,

---

[16] Milk and butter.

[17] Cornbread.

true to his bold nature, young Aurangzeb decided to make a statement. He donned a striking red gingham shirt, brown trousers and a hat perched jauntily on his head. To top it off, he borrowed his father's military bandana and wrapped it around his face, leaving just enough uncovered to maintain an air of mystery. Aurangzeb strode into the field with an exaggerated swagger and settled himself on a log, positioning himself conspicuously where his parents couldn't miss him. Hanief and Raj Begum stole amused glances at each other, trying their best to suppress their laughter and focus on their work. Minutes ticked by, and Aurangzeb's expectation of attention and reaction grew, yet his parents remained steadfastly focused on their harvest, ignoring his antics. Frustration brewed within Aurangzeb, but his pride kept him rooted to his spot, unwilling to admit defeat.

Finally, Mohammad Hanief couldn't resist the urge to tease his son. With a twinkle in his eye and a playful grin, he approached Aurangzeb, pretending to be serious. '*Begum, lagta hai bahar desh se mehmaan aaye hain, kuch chai nashta kara do*' (Begum, it seems we have esteemed guests from abroad. Please arrange for some refreshments), he joked, pulling the bandana down from Aurangzeb's face to reveal his bemused expression. Aurangzeb, torn between embarrassment and a desire to keep up the act, froze for a moment before slipping away from the scene, unnoticed by his amused parents.

As the sun dipped below the horizon and the day drew to a close, Hanief and Raj Begum returned home, only to discover that Aurangzeb had not returned since his dramatic display in the field. Hours passed, and their concern turned to worry as they searched frantically for their stubborn child, fearing the worst. Raj Begum's anxiety was increasing, and in her distress, she lashed out at Hanief, blaming him for laughing at Aurangzeb and driving him away. *'Sab aapki he galti hai. Aur hasso uss par. Ho gya na ab naraz'* (It is all your fault. You were laughing at him. Now he is angry somewhere). Hanief didn't know how to react. What was his fault? The foolish child dressed up as an Englishman while Hanief kept harvesting the crop all day, and, in the end, he only got flak for no fault of his. Maybe that's what being a 'husband' meant, he wondered.

As dusk settled over their house, a passerby heard an unusual rustling amidst the leaves of the Khubani tree just behind the property. The evening air was unusually calm, which further amplified the sound and stirred a hint of concern in the passerby. Upon shining his torch towards the branches, he was startled to find young Aurangzeb perched high up, static like an immovable object against the darkening sky. The man quickly called out to Mohammad Hanief, who, along with his family, was no stranger to Aurangzeb's dramatic escapades. They gathered beneath the tree, calling out to Aurangzeb, but he remained resolutely deaf to their pleas.

*'Hum isko poore gaon mein dhundh rahe hain aur yeh bewakoof yahan ped par baitha hai. Isko yahin chodh dete hain'* (We've searched all over the village for him, and this fool is enjoying himself up in a tree. Let's leave him here), Qasim remarked in frustration. At that moment, Mohammad Hanief could almost see Raj Begum's furious face flashing before his eyes. *'Nahin,'* (No), he countered swiftly, *'Isko ghar leke chalenge. Bahar kaafi thand ho rahi hai'* (Let's bring him home. It's getting cold out here).

Of course, deep down, Hanief wanted to side with Qasim, but the poor man feared Raj Begum's wrath way too much. 'Hanief, tujhe khud raat ko ped par rehna hai kya? (Do you want to spend the night on this tree?), he thought to himself, imagining the cold, uncomfortable prospect. 'Kabhi nahin!' (Not a chance!), he thought. Meanwhile, Aurangzeb, perched like a stubborn owl, was enjoying the spectacle far too much. He smirked mischievously, knowing fully well he had everyone wrapped around his little finger and was relishing the attention.

With his usual knack for diffusing tension, Qasim chimed in, 'Abbu, phir isko utarte hain isse pehle Ammi aag babula ho jayein. Varna aapko phir daant padegi' (Father, let's get him down before Ammi's temper reaches the boiling point. Otherwise, you will get scolded again!)

Hanief nodded vigorously, grateful for his son's diplomacy. 'Sahi bol raha hai Qasim! Aurangzeb neeche aa abhi' (You are right, Qasim! Aurangzeb, get down immediately), he called, trying to sound authoritative while secretly trying to avoid his wife's infamous lectures. True to his character, Aurangzeb remained stubbornly rooted at the spot. It wasn't until Qasim scaled the tree and gently nudged him that Aurangzeb relented. Hanief positioned himself below, ready to catch his son should he lose his balance.

Back on solid ground, Aurangzeb couldn't hide his smug grin. Deep down, despite his defiant exterior, he was secretly pleased to have finally garnered the attention he had sought all day.

Mohammad Hanief sighed inwardly, relieved yet exasperated by his son's antics. Aurangzeb's stubborn streak was as formidable as the roots of the Khubani tree, and for Hanief, navigating between his son's wilfulness and his wife's fiery temper often felt like tiptoeing through a minefield. Yet, in moments like these, amidst the laughter and annoyance, Hanief couldn't help but marvel at the spirited essence that made Aurangzeb who he was—a child determined to leave his mark on the world, even if it meant perching atop a tree in the fading light of the day.

Despite his stubbornness and dramatic flair, Aurangzeb remained the apple of his Ammi's eye. She could move mountains to fulfil all his erratic wishes. This pampered treatment often led Aurangzeb to believe he could achieve anything he set his mind to, regardless of his actual capabilities. One fine afternoon, as he strolled his way home from school with Qasim, Aurangzeb's attention was captivated by a group of military soldiers in sleek camouflage uniforms. Their disciplined demeanour and the allure of their uniform sparked a sudden declaration from Aurangzeb, '*Main toh fauj mein he jaunga. Vardi ki baat he kuch aur hai*' (I will join the Army. The uniform has its own charm).

Qasim couldn't resist teasing, '*Pehle ghar tak race mein toh hara ke dikha*' (First, try to defeat me in a race home). The challenge was accepted, and Aurangzeb set about proving his point. Little did he realize that his physique was more suited to enjoying his Ammi's lavish spread of white butter and jaggery than sprinting races. Upon reaching home, breathless but full of resolve, he proudly shared his newfound ambition with his father. Hanief, with a twinkle in his eye, chuckled softly before offering a fatherly nod of encouragement. '*Bilkul jaa sakte ho fauj mein. Par pehle dekh toh lein physically fit ho ki nahin*' (Of course, you can join the Army, but let's see if you're physically fit for it first), he remarked, gently testing Aurangzeb's resolve.

Dead set on proving himself, he accepted the challenge. Qasim and Hanief dragged a rope outside, stretched it across the path and set the stage for what would become a comedy of errors.

With a mischievous grin, Qasim teased, '*Chalo, chote bhai, tumhari fauji daud dekhte hain*' (Go on, little brother. Let's see your Army-worthy sprint).

Aurangzeb, buoyed by his determination and a dash of youthful exuberance, prepared for the leap. He rubbed his shoes on the ground to enhance his grip, mimicking the rituals he had seen in cricket matches. With the earnestness of a child lost in a daydream, he took off like a rocket. Although stubborn and full of big dreams, Aurangzeb was about as agile as a sack of potatoes. Instead of elegantly leaping over the rope, Aurangzeb managed to snag it with his foot in mid-air. With a mixture of surprise and horror, he continued forward, unintentionally dragging the rope along. His inevitable collision with the ground was less than graceful as he landed face-first in a cloud of dust. Qasim erupted into laughter, unable to contain his amusement at his brother's unexpected acrobatics.

Hanief, watching the scene unfold, also struggled to suppress his laughter. '*Itni fitness ke saath toh voh academy gate ke pass bhi nahi aane denge*' (With such agility, they might not even let you near the Academy gates), he joked.

Ammi, overhearing the commotion, rushed out with concern, only to find her beloved Aurangzeb covered in grass stains and a giggling Qasim. Aurangzeb, dusting himself off and ignoring the dirt smudges on his face, stood up bravely. '*Main kar sakta hoon. Ek chance aur dedo*' (I can do it! Just give me another chance).

His father, trying to keep a straight face, intervened, '*Beta, Army mein sirf josh se join nahi kar sakte. Physical fitness, discipline aur focus bhi chahiye'* (Son, joining the Army is not just about enthusiasm. It takes focus, agility and discipline).

Aurangzeb nodded as he absorbed ever word that Hanief spoke. He realized that becoming a soldier meant more than just wearing a snazzy uniform; it required hard work and focus. From that day on, he committed himself to a severe exercise routine under his father's watchful eye, determined to turn himself from a clumsy kid into a soldier worthy of his mother's unwavering support and his father's legacy. For Aurangzeb, the allure of the military uniform and his father's legacy were far more than mere fantasies—they were aspirations waiting to be fulfilled, one rope jump at a time.

Aurangzeb's home was like any other, brimming with the warmth of parental love, the cheerful sound of his siblings' laughter and the comforting aroma of home-cooked meals. The years passed swiftly, marking the growth of Aurangzeb and his siblings. Qasim, his elder brother, began to sport a faint moustache—a sign of approaching adulthood—while their parent's faces showed gentle traces of age and wisdom.

# #2

# The Girl at the Monsoon Fair

## 2009

As the years flowed by, Aurangzeb found himself shouldering new responsibilities. His family had grown, with younger brothers and sisters to look after. No longer the carefree youngster, he had matured into the role of an elder brother. Gone were the days of playful antics; now, discipline and responsibility defined his daily life. Time passed swiftly until it was Qasim's turn to pursue his lifelong ambition of following his father's footsteps and joining the Indian Army. Their father, Mohammad Hanief, had been the first individual from Salani village to don the olive-green uniform.

When Hanief made the bold choice to join the Indian Army, he didn't just embark on a personal journey—he ignited a spark of patriotism that spread like wildfire among Salani's youth. In years past, Salani had been a place overshadowed by turmoil and unrest, where the echoes of militant activities reverberated through the valleys. Hanief made this decision at a time when militants roamed the village streets openly and villagers feared not the militants but the military.

A beacon of hope and inspiration, his courage and unwavering determination cut through the darkness of uncertainty and rewrote the village's narrative.

Slowly but steadily, more young men and women from Salani followed Mohammad Hanief's example. They joined the armed forces, eager to defend their country and uphold its honour. Each recruit carried with them not just a uniform but the history of Salani's resilience and a determination to rise above its troubled past. Families who once feared for their safety found a newfound pride in their sons and daughters serving the nation.

Salani stood as a testament to the power of one man's courage. It had become one of those rare villages where every household had someone in uniform, ready to stand guard in some remote outpost, protect our borders or respond to crises. The village echoed with stories of sacrifice and service, and patriotism ran deep in the veins of its inhabitants. For Aurangzeb, seeing his father's legacy progress with Qasim's decision was a source of immense pride. As Qasim prepared for his journey into the Army, Aurangzeb did everything he could to support him. While he wasn't much help academically, Aurangzeb ensured Qasim stayed awake with warm milk late into the night. He could also be found at the village mosque every day, seeking blessings for his brother's journey.

Then, the long-awaited day arrived. News of Qasim's triumph in the written exams, physical tests and medical evaluations spread through the village like wildfire. Aurangzeb's heart swelled with pride and joy, bursting with emotions that words couldn't quite capture. Clutching the final merit list tightly in his hands, he ran through the dusty streets with the urgency of a man on a mission. Overflowing with happiness, Aurangzeb couldn't contain his sentiments. He shared sweets with everyone he met, his face beaming with an infectious smile. '*Abbu ki tarah Qasim bhi fauj main jaa raha hai aur jaldi main bhi jaunga*' (Like our father, Qasim is also going into the army and soon, I will too), he exclaimed proudly. With each word, his faith in his aspirations solidified. The journey that began with Mohammad Hanief's courage continued with Qasim's determination.

Time seemed to race forward like it was on roller skates. It felt like just yesterday when Qasim and Aurangzeb would playfully tease each other, with Qasim pulling his younger brother's leg and Aurangzeb sometimes showing his stubborn side. But now, Qasim was busy packing his bags, getting ready to leave home and start a new chapter in his life. It was a bittersweet moment for the entire family. '*Qasim, training mein khoob mehnat karna, best aana hai sab cheez mein*' (Qasim, work hard during your training, strive to be the best in everything), Aurangzeb said softly as he carefully folded Qasim's clothes. His voice carried a mixture of pride and concern, knowing the challenges that lay ahead for his older brother.

Eager to cherish every moment left in the village before his departure, Qasim replied enthusiastically, '*Haan haan, mehnat he karni hai iske baad. Shaam ko mela dekhne toh jaa rahe haina hum?*' (Yes, of course! I know I have to work hard after this but we're definitely going to the fair in the evening, right?)

'*Bilkul, har saal ki tarah sawan ke mahine ka mela thodi miss karenge*' (Absolutely, just like every year, we can't miss the monsoon fair), Aurangzeb affirmed warmly, a hint of nostalgia in his voice. The monsoon fair, locally known as

*Meander ke sawan ka mela,* was a highlight they all eagerly anticipated every year.

That evening, the atmosphere in their home was charged with a flurry of activity as Qasim and Aurangzeb, accompanied by their younger brothers Tariq, Shabbir, Zafar, Asim, and their sisters Shehnaaz and Shazia, got ready for the fair. They dressed impeccably, as if they were attending a grand wedding, each displaying their unique sense of style and swagger. The siblings took pride in dressing up for every occasion, big or small.

Meander buzzed with anticipation as the day of the mela dawned bright and sunny. Colourful banners fluttered in the gentle breeze, announcing the festivities that awaited. From early morning, the villagers bustled about, setting up stalls and decorating the fairground with streamers and lights. Children dashed around with excitement, their laughter echoing through the air. Aurangzeb and his siblings were among the first to arrive at the mela grounds. Their eyes widened with wonder at the sight of the bustling scene before them. Stalls lined the pathways adorned with golden trinkets and shimmering fabrics while the aroma of spicy snacks and sweet treats wafted temptingly through the air. The loud music emanating from the speakers all around added to the fervour. It was a celebration that every villager looked forward to each year.

'*Woh dekho!*' (Look at that!) Shehnaaz exclaimed, pointing to a stall filled with intricate papier mâché handicrafts. '*Mujhe Ammi ke liye kuch lena hai*' (I want to get something for mother). Qasim nodded, his gaze wandering to a stall selling freshly made kebabs. '*Kuch kha lein pehle. Bahot bhook lag rahi hai*' (Let's grab some food first. I'm starving!)

Aurangzeb was neither interested in food nor shopping. He would only come to the fair for the games and rides. Aurangzeb grinned mischievously. '*Par iske baad hum games khelenge. Iss baar toh prize lekar he jayenge*' (We'll hit the games after! I'm going to win the biggest prize this time). The gang eagerly made their way to the food stalls, where they indulged in crispy kebabs and fluffy naans and washed them down with glasses of refreshing apple juice. Energized and ready for adventure, they headed towards the game area, where colourful booths called out to them with promises of prizes and fun.

'*Jevi bhai, aap yeh wala game khelo. Mujhe toy chahiye*' (Jevi brother, you play this game. I want the toy), Shazia ran, pointing towards a game where the player had to toss rings onto bottles to win stuffed toys. Aurangzeb eagerly stepped up first, tossing the rings with precision. '*Bas ho gaya, ek shot aur*' (Almost got it! One more shot), he exclaimed as one of his rings narrowly missed its target. Shazia was eyeing the big blue teddy bear, and Aurangzeb would do anything to fulfil his little sister's wish. Such was their bond. All of them might fight when together, but in the outside world, they would stand like pillars of concrete, defending each other and working hard to fulfil each other's wishes. Soon, Qasim and Shabbir joined in, cheering each other on with every throw. After a few tries, they managed to win the fluffy teddy bear, which Shazia proudly hugged to her chest. Her day was made. She had already named him before they could reach the next stall. They all then proudly marched with their new fluffy friend, Dolu.

But the real excitement came when they spotted the towering Ferris wheel at the far end of the fairground. '*Woh dekho! Wahan chalte hain*' (Look there! Let's go there), Qasim declared, his eyes gleaming with enthusiasm. They hurried over. The ride at the fair was the most sought-after one, with people flooding the ticket counter to experience its thrill and joy. Aurangzeb quickly joined the queue of eager riders. For him, it was a tradition to go on the ride multiple times, as it gave him a rush of adrenaline. Aurangzeb couldn't help but feel a flutter of nerves in his stomach as they waited. He had always loved heights, but there was something exhilarating about being so high up in the air. Finally, it was their turn to climb into the brightly coloured iron gondolas. Aurangzeb and Qasim settled into one while Tariq and Shabbir rode the second one. Others were too young to ride, so they cheered their brothers from down below. Aurangzeb couldn't sit still— the excitement of the mid-air twirl of the gondola showed on his face. The Ferris wheel creaked into motion, slowly lifting them higher and higher. Aurangzeb leaned back in the swaying gondola, marvelling at the view. '*Wow! Kitna maza aa raha hai*' (Wow, this is a lot of fun), he exclaimed, his eyes wide with wonder. While Aurangzeb felt like he was flying in the air, a sight caught his attention. Across his gondola was a view he never thought he'd see up in the air. His eyes met beautiful, kohled, almond eyes, and he found himself captivated. Qasim nudged Aurangzeb teasingly. '*Toh, kaun hai voh jisse tabse ghoor raha hai?*' (So, who's the girl you are staring at?). Caught off guard, Aurangzeb blushed furiously. Across from him, in the gondola parallel to theirs, sat the girl with the beautiful eyes and smile. She wore a colourful scarf around her head, and her cheeks flushed with excitement as she smiled ear to ear, enjoying the ride. '*Voh, um, shayad mere school mein hai, pata nahi ek baar shayad dekha tha*' (Oh, um,

I think she's in our school. I'm not sure. I guess I saw her once in the school), Aurangzeb mumbled, unable to look away. Qasim grinned mischievously. '*Achaa! Lagta hai pasand aa gayi hain*' (Looks like someone's got a crush!). Aurangzeb rolled his eyes at Qasim's statement but couldn't resist stealing glances at the girl. There was something fascinating about her. It was either in the way her eyes sparkled with laughter or the way she waved at her friends with unabashed joy. She was like a breath of fresh air, her face as pretty as the dew drops on rose petals at dawn. As the Ferris wheel slowly rotated, Aurangzeb found himself lost in thought as he shyly tried to look at her from the side. What would it be like to talk to her? What does she sound like? Imagine hearing her laugh up close. Aurangzeb looked quite silly, smiling to himself. '*Zameen par aa gaye hain, utarna ka kasht karenge?*' (We have landed. Will you take the pain to get down?), Qasim wasn't missing a single chance to tease Aurangzeb.

The mela continued around them, alive with music, laughter and chatter. '*Ab Ammi ke liye kuch le lete hain*' (We should get something for Ammi now), Shehnaaz suggested as they walked away from the ride. 'Right,' Aurangzeb agreed, his mind still filled with thoughts of the girl on the Ferris wheel. They strolled through the mela again, selecting handmade jewellery and embroidered shawls for their mother. While everyone else was busy getting stuff, Aurangzeb couldn't help but scan the crowd, hoping to catch another glimpse of the girl who caught his attention. However, she seemed to have disappeared into the bustling crowd, leaving Aurangzeb with a strange longing and anticipation. Aurangzeb did believe that in matters of love, fate worked in mysterious ways. Of course, he didn't know what love felt like, but all he knew was that he wanted to see her again. And if God had the same plan, then their paths would definitely cross at a time when he would least expect it.

It was a very pleasant evening and a much-needed bonding time for the siblings before one of them left home. Soon, it was time for Qasim to leave for his training. So, with a bag packed with memories, Ammi's homemade delicacies and love, Qasim bid a tearful goodbye to his family. Aurangzeb and his father accompanied Qasim to the Meander bus stop. During the journey till there, Aurangzeb felt jittery and started asking Qasim about the stuff he had packed continuously, like a personal checklist. Qasim had to repeatedly remind him that he was the elder brother and not the other way around, but that was Aurangzeb. At the bus stop, Aurangzeb hugged his brother and wished him luck for this new chapter. He also told Qasim how he had big shoes to fill, following in his father's footsteps, and that he should do everything in his capacity to take the family name to greater heights. After Qasim's departure, Aurangzeb strolled the streets of Meander with his father. They met a lot of known people, bought grocery supplies for home, and had a much-needed father–son moment, especially now that one of them had left. Just then, Hanief came across Abdullah miya. 'Aurangzeb, yaad hai bachpan mein inse kabootar khareede the jo tumne saare uda diye the?' (Aurangzeb, remember we bought pigeons from him that you had set free?), Hanief laughed while greeting Abdullah miya. Aurangzeb was embarrassed. Why did parents have to bring up such awkward childhood memories in front of random people? Aurangzeb thought to himself. 'Aur, Hanief yahan kaise aana hua? Saaman lene aaya ho?' (And, Hanief, what brings you here? Are you here to get supplies?) Abdullah enquired. '*Nahi. Aaye toh Qasim ko chodne the. Uski fauj mein bharti ho gayi toh uski training ke liye gaya hai*' (No, we had come to drop Qasim. He has cleared his Army exam and has left for training). Hanief looked proud. '*Aap aaj kal dikhte kam ho Meander mein. Sab khairiyat?*' (I hardly see you in Meander these days. Hope all is well?) Hanief sat next to Abdullah at the tea stall. '*Mubarak ho janab. Bahot khoob. Haan, beta government clerk tha, abhi retire ho gaya hai, toh Salani laut aaye hain. Ab gaon mein he rehte hain*' (Congratulations Hanief, such lovely news. My son was a government clerk and is retired now. So, we have moved back to Salani. We now stay in the village), Abdullah directed the tea seller to give a cup to Hanief. '*Arey dekho, meri poti Ilham aa gayi. Chalo main ijazat leta hun*' (Oh! My granddaughter Ilham is here. I'll take your leave); Abdullah got up from the bench. Aurangzeb turned and saw the same girl walking towards him. He rubbed his eyes to make sure what he was seeing was real. '*As-salaam alaikum!*' Ilham greeted Hanief. Oh, dear god! The moment her sweet voice reached Aurangzeb, his heart filled with warmth. The sound of her voice was as peaceful as the gentle recitation of the Quran in a quiet room. Aurangzeb instantly looked towards her and smiled. He felt like a baby in a candy store, but this time he had to speak. God gave him another chance, but he might not get another after this.

While Hanief and Abdullah were busy discussing some village issues, Aurangzeb finally found the opportune moment to say a few words. '*Aap mela dekhne aaye the na?*' (You had come to see the fair, right?) Aurangzeb instantly regretted it. He could have initiated the conversation better. '*Aap mela dekhne aaye the ki mujhe?*' (Did you come to see the fair or me?), Ilham smiled and looked away. Aurangzeb blushed and chuckled softly. He was relieved that he could muster up the courage to strike up a conversation with Ilham. Her quick wit and charm had captivated him, and he could see himself engaging in a lively banter with her. Despite his initial nervousness, their conversation flowed effortlessly, as if they had known each other for years. He couldn't help but smile, feeling fortunate to have crossed paths with someone as delightful as Ilham at the village fair. They bid farewell with Aurangzeb's heart secretly wishing for another meeting soon.

Given the proximity of their homes, Aurangzeb and Ilham kept crossing paths. How come it took them so long to notice one another? Aurangzeb would often wonder. Their encounters became a delightful routine. Each meeting of theirs deepened their fondness for one another as they shared stories, laughter and quiet moments of understanding. As weeks turned into months, their friendship blossomed into something more. Aurangzeb found himself looking forward to seeing Ilham's bright smile and hearing her melodic laughter. Her presence brought a sense of joy and comfort that he cherished deeply. It was a feeling that was alien to Aurangzeb at first, unfamiliar yet exhilarating. He had never experienced such warmth and understanding with anyone before. Ilham's presence brought a sense of ease and acceptance that gradually melted his initial hesitation.

Ilham was this confident, bubbly girl with big dreams and plans. She seemed to live in a world straight out of a fairytale and approached life with a contagious enthusiasm that brightened every room she entered. She also spoke animatedly about her ambitions—travel the world, make a difference in her community and chase after dreams that others might deem too lofty. Her positivity was infectious, and she approached each day with a spirit that Aurangzeb found both inspiring and a little intimidating, if he were being honest.

In contrast, Aurangzeb was a young man of quiet determination and deep consideration, carrying the weight of his family's expectations on his shoulders. He was driven by a strong sense of duty to provide for and uplift his loved ones. His days would most often be filled with plans and strategies to secure a stable future for his family, often leaving little room for the whimsical dreams that Ilham embraced so freely. While he admired Ilham's zest for life, he sometimes felt overwhelmed by her boundless energy and optimism.

Yet, despite these differences, Aurangzeb couldn't help but be drawn towards Ilham's vibrant personality. Her laughter rang through the air like music, lifting his spirits and drawing him out of his shell. She would often encourage him to look beyond the confines of his responsibilities while nudging him gently to embrace spontaneity and the joy of living in the present moment. 'Life isn't that long—we must appreciate every moment,' was Ilham's philosophy. For Ilham, Aurangzeb was an anchor to her wandering mind and limitless aspirations. She felt safe with him. His calm demeanour and compassionate support gave her the stability she needed to pursue her dreams confidently. He listened attentively to her plans and goals, offering practical advice and a steady hand to guide her through life's challenges. She had never encountered a man who took so much interest in her dreams or was ready to stand next to her, silent yet strong.

'*Kya? Tumhe fauj mein jana hai? Vahan toh khatra bohot hota hai na?*' (What? You want to join the Indian Army? Isn't that risky?) Ilham's voice was tinged with worry. '*Arey, apne desh ki sewa karne mein kya khatra. Aur jiske saath tum ho, usse toh maut bhi daregi. Tum chodogi thodi agar mujhe kuch hua toh*' (There is no risk in serving your nation. On top of that, I have you. Even death would be scared to harm me knowing you are there), Aurangzeb tried to inject some humour. '*Toh kab jaa rahe ho?*' (So, when are you leaving?) she whispered sadly. '*Mere chacha ki fauj thodi hai. Pehle toh exam clear karna padega. Pata hai kitna mushkil hai?*' (The Army doesn't belong to my family. I need to clear the exam first. You know how difficult that is?) Aurangzeb laughed. '*Mujhe kaise pata hoga? Humare yahan koi fauj mein nahi hai*' (How would I know? Nobody from my family is in the Army), Ilham wasn't pleased with his humour.

Aurangzeb then explained the entire selection process to Ilham—he thought she needed to know the hurdles and challenges he would face on his path to his dream. He told her he would first apply online on the Indian Army website. An all-India level written examination called the Indian Army Common Entrance Examination (CEE) would have to be cleared, and clearing the exam was no easy feat. Aurangzeb shared with Ilham that he would have to brush up on his general knowledge, mathematics, logical reasoning and English. For a boy who had studied Urdu and Hindi all his life, and who had to first think in Urdu, then translate the same in his head in Hindi and then further translate it into broken English before uttering the words, this was a mammoth challenge. Of course, in case he was fortunate enough to clear the written exam, he would have to undergo a rigorous physical test, involving a timed 1.6 km-run that needed to be finished in less than five-and-a-half minutes.

The physical test also involved ten pull-ups, jumping over a 9-foot trench and zig-zag balance walking. This stage checked the candidate's physical endurance, strength and agility—not a cakewalk by any measure. Ilham's head was already spinning, but that wasn't the end. In case he managed to qualify for the above two stages, he would have to go through a detailed medical examination, and would receive his joining letter only if he was medically fit as per military standards. While explaining the selection process, Aurangzeb took pleasure in observing Ilham's expressions as they shifted from curiosity to concern and finally, to pure horror upon hearing about the strenuous and lengthy process involved.

'*Tum chinta mat karo. Abhi toh Qasim bhai ki kasam parade hogi, aur unke nikaah ki bhi baat chal rahi hai. Meri bharti mein abhi time hain aur main kahin nahi jaa raha hoon*' (You need not worry. Brother Qasim will be getting commissioned soon, and talks are being held about his marriage as well. There is a lot of time before I join the Army, and I am not leaving you and going anywhere). Saying this, Aurangzeb held Ilham's hand, which she had comfortably rested on her lap. The moment Aurangzeb's hand touched the back of her palm, a gentle breeze seemed to stir around them, carrying faint notes of azaan. Ilham looked at him, surprised but comforted by his touch. Aurangzeb felt a deep connection growing between them as if it was the beginning of something special—their forever maybe. Ilham could never have imagined that the young boy she first saw in her grandfather's shop, picking out pigeons for his birthday, would one day hold the strings to her heart. It seemed like a dream unfolding, like fate had quietly woven their paths together. Every glance, every smile they exchanged now carried a meaning; a tender connection that grew stronger with each passing day. In Aurangzeb's eyes, she found comfort and understanding; in his touch, she felt a gentle blanket of security. Their journey from strangers to this moment felt like a magical tale, where the ordinary had transformed into something extraordinary—a love story written in the simplest of gestures and the quietest of whispers. '*Chalo kaafi late ho gaya, Ammi raah dekh rahi hongi*' (It's getting late, I should leave. My mother must be expecting me any minute now), Ilham got up with a contented smile playing on her lips. Aurangzeb hated saying goodbye to her, but he didn't quite have a choice. With a heavy heart, he bid her farewell. As Ilham's steps moved away from Aurangzeb, she stopped abruptly. '*Suno, birthday pe kabootar kaun khareedta hai?*' (Listen, who buys pigeons as their birthday present?) Ilham laughed and resumed her journey home. This girl would always catch Aurangzeb off guard. He hit his palm on his head and laughed. She remembered him from years ago. He wasn't the only one who was enamoured by her beauty, maybe his silly antics caught her attention as well.

While Aurangzeb's heart soared with happiness, his family was equally joyous. Hanief and Raj Begum were returning with Qasim after attending his passing out parade.[18] As Hanief and Raj Begum returned home, their hearts swelled with pride. The atmosphere at Aurangzeb's home buzzed with jubilation as the parents recounted the solemnity and grandeur of the occasion. Hanief's eyes shone with admiration as he spoke

---

[18] A solemn ceremony that marks an individual's journey from a recruit to a soldier. Every individual enters their respective training centres with dreams in their eyes and proudly exits donning the olive-green uniform after taking the oath that the nation is supreme—above everyone and everything.

of Qasim's impeccable drill and the crispness of his uniform, which showed how dedicated Qasim was and the amount of hard work he had put in during his time in the academy. Raj Begum, wiping away tears of joy, shared anecdotes of the emotional moments when they saw Qasim marching with his comrades, embodying the values of honour and duty. The home was filled with the fragrance of garlands and the aroma of celebratory sweets as they all encircled Qasim to hear the tales of the academy. Celebrations cascaded through Hanief's household as, following Qasim's splendid passing out parade from the Indian Army, the family embraced another joyous occasion—the *nikaah*.[19] While Qasim was going through the rigorous training, during one of his term breaks, his marriage was arranged with a beautiful girl named Rubeena who was also from Salani. The family couldn't wait to welcome the new member.

Back in the day, when homes didn't have bathrooms, open defecation was a common practice. Everyone used lotas to carry water for their daily needs. It was expected to see villagers lining up each morning and making their way to the open fields. Aurangzeb found humour in the situation and would playfully tease Qasim about how, ever since his marriage to Rubeena was arranged, Qasim seemed to be carrying his lota in the direction of her house every morning. *'Lagta hai intezaar nahi ho raha Rubeena ko dobara dekhne ka'* (Looks like you can't wait to see Rubeena again), Aurangzeb would chuckle, and they'd share a laugh over Qasim's supposed eagerness to be married to Rubeena. The teasing

---

[19] Marriage as per Muslim rituals.

became a daily ritual, turning what was once a mundane task into a light-hearted joke between the brothers.

Finally, it was the day of the nikaah, and Mohammad Hanief's modest courtyard was transformed into a fragrant oasis adorned with strings of jasmine and roses. The air was alive with the sweet scent of flowers as colourful fabric canopies hung overhead, twinkling with the delicate strings of fairy lights. Qasim, the centre of attention on that momentous day, sat nervously under the canopy of flowers. Dressed impeccably in a pristine white kurta–pajama paired with an embroidered golden waistcoat, he exuded royalty, though his face screamed anxiousness. As he awaited the arrival of his bride-to-be, Qasim's emotions played out visibly. His fingers drummed lightly on his knees, displaying his nervous energy even though he was trying very hard to appear composed. His gaze frequently drifted towards the entrance of the courtyard, where Rubeena would soon make her entrance. The courtyard hummed with the gentle murmur of guests arriving and exchanging greetings, punctuated by the soft tunes playing on the speaker. Family members and close friends gathered around Qasim, offering words of encouragement and reassurance, their faces reflecting pride and joy for the young man about to embark on a new chapter of his life. In this moment suspended in time, amidst the blossoming flowers and twinkling lights, Rubeena walked in looking like a dream. She wore a red and gold lehenga, with her face modestly veiled.

The two settled across one another, divided by an intricate knit of jasmine flowers. The imam[20] proceeded with

---

[20] Imam is a religious leader in Islam who has multiple roles, including leading prayers, teaching the Quran and officiating at weddings and funerals.

the rituals of the nikaah, asking Qasim thrice, '*Qubool hai?*' (Do you accept?), to which Qasim responded affirmatively each time, his voice steady with conviction. Rubeena, seated beside her mother, listened attentively as her consent was sought and given in the traditional manner. As the imam solemnly conducted the ceremony, Aurangzeb found himself captivated by Ilham's presence. She looked absolutely radiant in her summer-yellow salwar kameez, adorned with delicate embroidery. The fading sunlight caught the edges of her dupatta, casting a soft glow that illuminated her face, making her appear like a vision of sunshine amidst the gathering. For Aurangzeb, everything else faded into the background as his gaze lingered on Ilham. Her grace and beauty seemed to mesmerize him, and in that moment, he wished he could declare his feelings and whisper 'Qubool hai' to her. Yet, he knew this was not his moment; it belonged to Qasim and Rubeena, whose union was being blessed by prayers. Despite the swirl of emotions within him, Aurangzeb watched silently, his heart admiring Ilham from afar as her presence cast a spell on him that he couldn't easily shake off. Amidst the recitations and prayers, the assembled guests showered blessings upon the couple, each one offering heartfelt wishes for a prosperous and harmonious marital journey.

The household brimmed with newfound joy as Rubeena became a part of the family. However, soon after the nikaah, Qasim departed for his duty station, leaving his new bride behind with a heavy heart. Over time, Rubeena grew very fond of the family, especially Aurangzeb, who looked after her like an older brother and was always there to guide and support her. Aurangzeb made sure that Rubeena knew she could rely on him. He told her that she could talk to him if she ever felt unsure or lonely while Qasim was away on duty. He promised to treat her just like Shehnaaz or Shazia, ensuring she felt loved and valued in the household. These words meant a lot to Rubeena. They eased her worries about being alone when Qasim wasn't there. Aurangzeb's kindness and support became her rock, giving her strength and comfort in a place that was still unfamiliar. With Aurangzeb's encouragement, Rubeena faced each day with more confidence, knowing she had someone caring, like a brother, to lean on through the ups and downs of married life. What more could a young girl want from her in-laws' house other than acceptance and love? When a girl leaves her home and walks the unfamiliar path blindly trusting a man, she doesn't want jewels or a piece of land, but a place in the family where she could stand. For Rubeena, these were the pillars of her happiness in her new home. From the moment she stepped into the household as Qasim's bride, Rubeena felt a mix of nerves and excitement. The unfamiliar surroundings and new faces could have been daunting, but the warmth and welcome she received melted away any apprehensions. Aurangzeb often reminded her that she was not just a daughter-in-law but a cherished family member, worthy of the same love and respect as anyone else. His words of reassurance became a constant source of comfort for Rubeena, especially during moments of homesickness or uncertainty. The family, too, embraced Rubeena wholeheartedly. They showered her with affectionate gestures, from preparing her favourite dishes to including her in family gatherings, celebrations and also in moments of serious family discussions. She was one of them and she never felt otherwise. Their acceptance of Rubeena as one of their own filled her heart with gratitude and a sense of belonging. In return, Rubeena poured her heart into making her new household a home. She brought warmth and positivity into every corner, contributing to the household chores and bonding with each family member. Her efforts were met with admiration and appreciation, further solidifying the bonds of love and acceptance that had blossomed since her arrival. For Rubeena, acceptance and love were not just words but the foundation upon which she built her new life. In the embrace of her in-laws' affection and Aurangzeb's unwavering support, she found the happiness and security she had always hoped for in her married life. Aurangzeb's approach towards Rubeena revealed his kind heart. He showed that one doesn't need degrees to treat a girl, who is joining a new family, with respect and care. All it takes is an open heart and genuine kindness, a kindness so profound that it can be felt by all, can be seen by the blind, and heard by the deaf.

As days passed, Aurangzeb immersed himself in preparing for his upcoming exams, feeling the weight of responsibility on his shoulders. Amidst the stress and busyness of his life, Aurangzeb found solace in glimpses of Ilham's smile. Her radiant expression became his daily dose of comfort, a bright spot that eased his worries and lifted his spirits. Whether in passing moments or brief encounters, even if he had a few minutes to spare in the middle of his preparations, he wouldn't miss a chance to see Ilham. As days passed, the rhythm of their lives continued to unfold. Aurangzeb got embroiled in his household responsibilities, exams and daily routine. His hushed meetings with Ilham were reduced to half, but his love for her leapt with each passing day. By sheer hard work and determination, Aurangzeb navigated through all the stages of his Army entrance exam. Despite the hurdles, he persevered with unwavering dedication, fuelled by his childhood dream of serving his country.

All that was left was the anxiety of the impending result. Every day, Aurangzeb's routine included rushing to get the newspaper, his heart pounding with anticipation as he would turn page after page to read the news of the result. Finally, the most anticipated day arrived. As Aurangzeb scanned the newspaper, his hands trembled slightly, hoping to see his name among the successful candidates. Time seemed to slow down as he searched through the pages and each passing moment was filled with hope and anxiety. The weight of years of hard work and dedication hung heavy on his shoulders as he yearned for positive news. When his eyes finally landed on his name, which was listed among those who had cleared all stages of the exam, a rush of emotions flooded through Aurangzeb—joy, relief and a profound sense of accomplishment washed over him all at once. Tears streamed down his face—that young boy who couldn't jump across the rope had achieved his dream and made it into reality. Aurangzeb felt like the bird released from the cage into the open sky. He rushed to his parents with moist eyes and a smile so bright that it could light up the darkest night. His father, lazing under the Khubani tree, looked up at the sound of hurried steps. As their eyes met, Aurangzeb's excitement was contagious. Without a word, he embraced his father tightly, feeling the warmth of pride and love in the returned embrace. Hanief knew that Aurangzeb was no longer the stubborn young boy who would climb the same Khubani tree and throw tantrums; he was now hugging a young man ready to serve his country and take his family legacy forward. His mother, bustling in the kitchen, turned around at the sound of their laughter, her eyes misting with tears of joy as she saw the enthusiasm painted on Aurangzeb's face. In a rush of emotions, Aurangzeb recounted every detail of his journey to success. His father listened intently, while a mix of admiration and happiness reflected in his eyes. His mother wiped away tears of pride as she hugged him again, whispering words of love and appreciation.

Aurangzeb couldn't wait to share the news with Ilham. His heart raced as he rushed to find her. Each step felt like a leap towards sharing his triumph with someone who had become his confidante and supporter in a very short span of time. Finally reaching her, he couldn't hide his excitement. His words tumbled out in a rush of joy and relief. *'Ilham, kar diya maine. Exam clear kar liya'* (Ilham, I did it! I cleared the exam!), he exclaimed; his voice heavy with emotion. He knelt on the ground and heaved a sigh of relief. Ilham's eyes widened with delight, mirroring Aurangzeb's contagious happiness. She squealed with joy, hugging him tightly as if his success was her personal victory. Her face lit up with pride and admiration and her heart swelled with happiness for him. She said, *'Mujhe toh pehle se pata tha'* (I knew you could do it) and did a little celebratory dance of her own. At that moment, as they shared Aurangzeb's triumph, their bond grew even stronger. It wasn't just about his achievement— it was about the shared journey they had embarked upon together, supporting each other through challenges and celebrating each milestone. In that fleeting moment, amidst the celebrations and congratulations, Ilham grappled with the poignant truth that Aurangzeb's triumph marked the beginning of a journey that could lead them on diverging paths. She smiled warmly at him, her heart genuinely filled with pride and happiness for his achievement. Yet, beneath that smile, a quiet ache settled in. Aurangzeb's success meant their everyday interactions would soon become memories rather than realities. No longer would she experience the comfort of his presence, the sound of his voice or the shared laughter they often took for granted. It would soon be a luxury she might not be able to afford regularly. Deep within, Ilham knew that each passing day would only draw them further apart. Hereon, she cherished every mundane moment they spent together, recognizing its value as the glue that bound their connection. From that moment on, Ilham held every second she spent in Aurangzeb's presence dear to her heart. She found herself noticing the small details—the way his eyes crinkled when he laughed, the sound of his voice when he spoke passionately about his dreams and the warmth of his hand when they walked side by side. Only if she could speak to him a little longer or hold him for a moment more—there was no end to such thoughts. The inevitability of the matter was that Aurangzeb would walk away physically; she just had to treasure him in her heart permanently.

# #3

# Covert Operation: The Narrow Escape

## 2011

The day Ilham had always dreaded had arrived—it was time for Aurangzeb to leave. He bid adieu to his family and Ilham, and with a heavy heart, moved towards the Jammu and Kashmir Light Infantry Regimental Centre at Srinagar. This had been Aurangzeb's dream since he was a little boy, and throughout his journey, he couldn't believe that it was unfolding into reality. The foundation of the Jammu and Kashmir Light Infantry Regiment is intertwined with India's first war after Independence. In 1947–48, when the Kaballis,[21] with the support of Pakistan, attacked India, a regiment under the name Jammu and Kashmir Militia came into existence to defend the Indian frontiers. A volunteer force by design, the J&K Militia successfully pushed back the intruders and established peace. They fought bravely during the 1962, 1965, 1971 and 1999 Kargil war and won accolades. With several military honours and theatre honours

---

[21] Tribesmen.

to its name, it became one of the most decorated regiments of the Indian Army. Owing to the tales of bravery attached to its name, the force was called the Jammu and Kashmir Light Infantry Regiment since April 1976.

Standing before the Centre, Aurangzeb felt a sense of honour and respect. This was it. This was his dream. The sun shining bright on the red and white minaret-style main gate with Chuni Lal Dwar embossed in silver made Aurangzeb smile with relief. The air inside the Regimental Centre was not just a medium for breathing but a living proof of the dedication, sacrifice and resolute spirit that defined those who chose to wear the uniform. It was an atmosphere where ordinary individuals were forged into extraordinary soldiers, ready to face the challenges of today and tomorrow with unwavering courage and unflinching pride. In those barracks, under the same flag, stood individuals from bustling metropolises and serene hamlets alike. Each soldier brought their own story and experiences, yet within those walls, all were bound by a common dedication to duty and service. It didn't matter if you were a farmer's son or the scion of a business magnate, a scholar or a tradesman. What mattered was the shared commitment to upholding the values of honour, courage and unity. Behind 'Unity Lines,' respect was earned through sweat and effort, not through titles or lineage. Every soldier, from the greenest recruit to the seasoned veteran, found their place in this tapestry of camaraderie and shared sacrifice. The main gate also had 'Unity Lines' written on either side, which meant that everyone was equal behind these ginormous iron gates irrespective of their religion, caste, creed or background. It was a place where differences were celebrated as strengths and bonds forged in adversity transcended barriers of creed and circumstance. Within those walls, 'Unity Lines' stood not just as a phrase but a living testament to the power of unity in diversity—a reminder that in the face of challenges, they were strongest when they stood together, shoulder to shoulder, as one unified force. Even the first stone laid to construct the Regimental Centre had the words 'Unity Lines' engraved on it—it still adorns one of the roundabouts in the Regimental Centre.

It was a new environment for Aurangzeb. He had never ventured out of Poonch, and here he was, living with people from different communities and ethnicities. The Regimental Centre was also home to a multi-faith prayer hall where recruits would congregate to celebrate their diversity. Inside the multi-faith prayer hall at the Regimental Centre, the atmosphere was a harmonious blend of devotion and mutual respect, reflecting the diversity of the recruits. Regardless of their religious background, each soldier felt comfortable and respected within the prayer hall, where their individual beliefs were honoured and embraced. It was not uncommon to witness a Muslim recruit deeply engaged in reciting verses from the Bhagavad Gita, exploring the wisdom and teachings revered by Hindus. At the same time, a Hindu soldier could be found singing the verses of Gurbani, immersing himself in the spiritual hymns cherished by Sikhs. Meanwhile, a Sikh recruit would bow in prayer, offering supplications to Allah. These moments of interfaith interaction were more than just displays of tolerance; they embodied a genuine spirit of understanding and acceptance among the recruits. At the Regimental Centre, Aurangzeb encountered a profound lesson in unity that transcended superficial differences. Accustomed to the familiar sweetness of seviyaan,[22] a dish rooted in his upbringing, he gradually discovered a deeper appreciation for the communal essence and simplicity embodied in kada prasad.[23] A humble offering in Sikh tradition, the kada prasad became more than just a food item for Aurangzeb; it symbolized the spirit of sharing and equality that resonated deeply within the Regiment. As is tradition, in the Jammu and Kashmir Light Infantry Regiment, commonly called JAK LI Regiment, every section[24] of every platoon of every company depicted India in its entirety. A section would have four Hindu recruits, four Muslim recruits and two Sikhs—a strength of ten soldiers that embodied the ideals and aspirations that define the true essence of the Preamble of the Indian Constitution. Aurangzeb adjusted seamlessly to his new life, though he had his moments where he might shed a tear or two at night, missing his home and heart.

In the Academy, Aurangzeb was taught counter-insurgency training with case studies, rock climbing that would aid him in mountainous terrain and bayonet fighting, a close combat fight that is essential for a soldier. War-like simulations would be created where recruits would be taught personal camouflage and concealments on the ground through which they could go as close as possible to the enemy and neutralize them. Not to forget the lifeline of any training academy—the drill. The drill

---

[22] A dessert made with milk, sugar and vermicelli.

[23] A religious offering mainly given in gurudwaras (Sikh place of worship) made of wheat flour, ghee and sugar.

[24] Every section had a strength of ten soldiers. Three sections together make a platoon. Three or four platoons taken together is a company.

plays a crucial role in military training by instilling discipline, precision and cohesion among soldiers. The uniformity achieved enhances overall unit coordination and effectiveness, ensuring soldiers can operate seamlessly as an organized team. Additionally, drills contribute to physical fitness and endurance, building the strength and stamina necessary for the rigours of military service. Aurangzeb would look forward to drill practices as that was the only time their faces were not caked with mud and their uniforms were crisply ironed.

While Aurangzeb swung through the endless drills and punishments at the Academy, he found solace in Ilham's letters. Each word penned was a whisper of longing— evidence of her love that bridged the distance between them. Her letters spoke of dreams where she held him close, imagining the touch of his hand and the warmth of his smile. For Aurangzeb, reading Ilham's letters was like being wrapped in a warm blanket. Her words were not just ink on paper but whispers of love that filled his heart with longing and happiness. They reminded him of the love waiting for him in Salani, a love that made the hardships of academy life feel insignificant. Aurangzeb cherished each letter as if it were a treasure, a precious reminder of their deep connection and the dreams they shared for their future together. In those fleeting moments of solitude, amidst the demands of his training, Aurangzeb would close his eyes and imagine being with Ilham, holding her close and sharing their hopes and dreams. Her letters were his lifeline, guiding him through each day with a renewed sense of purpose and determination. They were his source of strength, filling him with gratitude for the love that anchored him amidst the turbulence of military life. Despite his deep affection for Ilham, Aurangzeb struggled to find time to reply. The Academy's demanding schedule left little room for personal correspondence, much to Ilham's playful dismay. In her letters, she would tease him about his 'second love affair' with his drill instructor, imagining him dodging push-ups and chores as he might try to steal a moment to write back. The irony wasn't lost on Aurangzeb as he found himself caught between the discipline of military life and the tender demands of love. He often joked with his comrades about his 'toughest battle,' the one he wasn't fighting on the training ground, but in finding time to write back to his beloved in the middle of the relentless demands of military life.

## 2012

Time seemed to fly for Aurangzeb as the day of his passing out parade approached, now just a fortnight away. He eagerly anticipated the moment when his parents would stand proudly at the centre, watching him march on the prestigious Bana Singh Ground. As he practised his drills and polished his uniform, Aurangzeb envisioned the pride in his parents' eyes as their unwavering support and love propelled him toward this significant milestone in his military journey. Every step he took was fuelled by the desire of making them proud and fulfilling his childhood dream. Aurangzeb had always had a keen eye on what his family wore, and for this special day, he insisted they wear their finest attire. He especially asked his Ammi to bring along Kud ki mithai, a famous flaky dessert soaked in pure ghee that he cherished and wanted to share with his fellow recruits. The night before the passing out parade was restless for Aurangzeb. Excitement fluttered in his stomach, making it hard to sleep even for a moment.

Thoughts of the upcoming day filled his mind—the pride of marching on the revered Bana Singh Ground, the thrill of showcasing his skills and the joy of seeing his parents' faces beaming with pride.

On the morning of the parade, Aurangzeb stood resplendent in his finest attire—a crimson regimental *pagdi*[25] gracing his head, the olive-green uniform adorned with a cummerbund in regimental colours. His white gloves and anklets added a striking contrast, breaking the monotony of the earthy tones. As the recruits seamlessly marched onto the prestigious Bana Singh Ground, every movement of their hands and legs was synchronized, displaying the precision and discipline instilled in them during training. As Aurangzeb marched with determination thumping his direct moulded sole (DMS) boots on the charcoal tarmac, his heart overflowed with happiness. As he reached the culmination of the parade, a sense of accomplishment washed over him like a gentle wave embracing the shore. The applause and cheers from the audience reverberated like a symphony of celebration, marking the completion of one chapter and the beginning of another in his military career. In that moment, Aurangzeb knew that his dedication, sacrifice and unflinching spirit had brought him to this pinnacle of success. He stood tall, ready to embrace the challenges and adventures that lay ahead in his journey to serve his country in the Indian Army.

Aurangzeb's transformation from a young man to a soldier of the Indian Army was a leap of courage and dedication. With the motto *Balidanam Veer Lakshanam* (Sacrifice is the hallmark of the brave), he embraced his olive-green uniform

---

[25] Turban.

with profound pride. At the Regimental Centre, as the war cry 'Bharat Mata Ki Jai' echoed, tears welled up in the eyes of onlookers, moved by the solemnity and significance of the moment. The highlight of the day came when Hanief and Raj Begum, with hearts brimming with pride, placed the olive flannel beret adorned with his regiment's insignia upon Aurangzeb's head. It symbolized not just his achievement, but the honour and responsibility he now carried as a soldier. Returning to Salani after his commissioning, Aurangzeb felt a sense of transformation. His shoulders bore the weight of accomplishment, and he carried himself with newfound confidence. For the first time, he truly felt that he had achieved something significant, and the villagers greeted him with admiration and warmth. Their pride in him was palpable, a reflection of the respect and esteem he had earned through his hard work and selfless service to the nation. As he stood amidst the familiar faces and voices of his villagers, Aurangzeb knew that he had found his purpose. The journey from an aspiring recruit to a commissioned soldier shaped him into a person of strength and integrity. He was now ready to face the challenges ahead with the same determination that had brought him to this proud moment—a moment that marked not just his personal achievement, but a commitment to uphold the values and ideals of the Indian Army with honour and pride.

Aurangzeb eagerly anticipated Ilham's reaction to seeing him in his olive-green uniform. It had been months since they last met, and he couldn't wait to be reunited with the woman whose presence made his heart race. Standing near the edge of a nearby cliff, his eyes scanned the surroundings, longing to catch a glimpse of her familiar face. When Ilham finally appeared, her heart skipped a beat at the sight of

Aurangzeb in uniform for the first time. He looked every bit the soldier she had imagined him to be—tall and proud, with a demeanour that spoke of courage and determination. A new sense of purpose radiated from him.

Aurangzeb's eyes lit up as Ilham drew near. He couldn't help but smile, feeling relief and joy at finally reuniting with her. He reached out to take her hand, his touch gentle yet firm. They stood together in silence, surrounded by the beauty of nature and the quiet strength of their love. In that serene moment, they knew that no matter the distance or challenges, they were united in their journey. Though months had passed, nothing changed between them, except the fact that they clearly understood their feelings for one another. The three magical words had never been spoken but were felt every second, every minute apart. As they gazed into each other's eyes, a sense of peace washed over them, reassuring them that their bond was strong and their love was enduring. He was finally home, but not for long.

Aurangzeb had proven himself as the best shooter at the academy with his hard work and natural flair. And so, before joining his unit, 4 Jammu and Kashmir Light Infantry (4 JAK LI), he headed to Bangalore for a big tournament. He had chosen this life for himself—whenever duty called, he had to leave home and his loved ones behind in a heartbeat.

Life in the military soon became routine, with postings from one place to another. Even as Aurangzeb lived his dream of serving in the Army, there were moments when nostalgia tugged at his heart, yearning for the familiar comforts of home. He longed for the comfort of resting his head on Ammi's lap and the peaceful moments of watching sunsets with Ilham. Military life felt like sailing uncharted seas, where every task presented before him fresh challenges and chances to grow stronger. Throughout it all, memories of his family and the love of Ilham anchored him, providing solace amid the uncertainties of his career. His dedication to duty burned brightly within him, fuelled by a profound sense of pride and responsibility.

Aurangzeb understood that each obstacle he encountered was a stepping stone on his path to becoming the finest soldier he could be. As he forged ahead in his military journey, he carried with him the wisdom gained from both the academy and the field, as each day brought new trials and opportunities to prove his mettle. He remained resolute in his commitment, knowing that every endeavour contributed to a cause greater than himself. In the quiet moments between duties, thoughts of home and loved ones brought him strength and motivation. With every sunrise and every completed mission, Aurangzeb found fulfilment in serving his nation, driven by a sense of purpose that transcended mere duty and became a heartfelt calling.

Even though the Indian Army was his first love, Aurangzeb had a special place reserved just for Ilham. She wasn't just a part of his life; she was his life. Her presence was like a comfort blanket where Aurangzeb could lower his guard, be vulnerable and share his dreams and fears without hesitation. Ilham's love reminded him of life beyond the Army, grounding him in the reality of human connection amidst the disciplined world of military service. Life for Aurangzeb and his parents was moving on the right path—there couldn't be anyone as proud as Hanief and Raj Begum, whose two sons were serving the Indian Army in different parts of the country.

* * *

In 2016, Aurangzeb moved on deputation from 4 JAK LI to 44 Rashtriya Rifles at Shopian. He became part of the Shadimarg post company of 44 Rashtriya Rifles. Aurangzeb was rather excited about his posting order—Shopian was hardly four hours away from Salani and he felt that he was moving closer to home. When he reached his new company location, Aurangzeb was briefed about the volatile situation in their area of responsibility and the dos and don'ts of being part of Rashtriya Rifles. The Rashtriya Rifles (RR) is a specialized force within the Indian Army, established in 1990 to combat insurgency and terrorism in Jammu and Kashmir. Tasked with conducting counter-terrorism operations, RR units operate under the operational control of the Indian Army and are trained extensively in counter-insurgency tactics, jungle warfare and intelligence gathering. Comprising troops from various army units, RR personnel are equipped with modern weaponry and equipment suited for their challenging missions. Beyond military operations, RR units engage in community outreach and humanitarian efforts to foster stability and trust among local populations. Over the years, they have played a pivotal role in stabilizing the security situation in the region, contributing significantly to efforts to restore peace and normalcy.

Aurangzeb quickly learned that the Rashtriya Rifles unit he joined was highly active and regularly engaged in operations and encounters with militants in his home state. His passion for joining the Indian Army was driven by a deep-seated desire to protect the honour of the Indian flag and defend his country against those who sought to undermine it. Anybody who dared to tarnish the glory of the Indian tricolour was an enemy in his eyes. However, it became particularly challenging for Aurangzeb as he often found himself confronting militants who were from his own state. It is difficult fighting militants on a daily basis but imagine a soldier who is torn between the oath and his people. Aurangzeb had to fight his own people for his country. Despite these challenges, Aurangzeb saw an opportunity to turn the tide. He understood the importance of not just fighting militants but also inspiring the youth of his state to choose the path of joining the Indian military rather than taking up arms against it. He believed in leading by example, demonstrating through his actions and dedication, how serving in the Army could bring honour, respect and a meaningful way to contribute to the nation. For Aurangzeb, every operation was not just about eliminating threats but also about fostering a sense of pride and unity amongst the people that he had sworn to protect. He knew that by engaging with local communities, listening to their concerns and showing empathy, he could win their trust and support in the fight against insurgency. His goal was to secure physical territory and reclaim the hearts and minds of his fellow citizens, convincing them that the path of peace and progress lay in unity under the Indian flag. In this way, Aurangzeb saw his role in the Rashtriya Rifles as more than that of a soldier—to him, it was a calling to bridge divides, promote understanding, and build a brighter future for his state and his country.

Aurangzeb had grown his hair and beard to blend in with the local populace, a common practice among soldiers posted in counter-insurgency areas. Interestingly, his new look had a particular humorous tale to it that Qasim fondly narrates to everyone even today.

Once when he was home on leave, Aurangzeb decided
to venture out with Ammi and Qasim. During the outing,
he decided to stop at a nearby army canteen to purchase
supplies. It was a typical day, with Aurangzeb dressed casually
in civilian clothes, his charcoal black locks swept across his
face and he had a well-maintained beard. As they approached
the canteen, he, eager to help his mother and brother, entered
first. The atmosphere inside the canteen was vibrant, with
soldiers and veterans alike going about buying groceries.
Aurangzeb's presence, while intended to be inconspicuous,
unexpectedly drew attention. Two women, startled by his
appearance, mistook him for a militant who had supposedly
infiltrated the army area. In a flurry of panic, the women
hurried out of the canteen, their voices raised in alarm, alerting
others to the perceived security breach. Their cries echoed
through the compound, causing a momentary commotion
among those nearby. For Aurangzeb's family, who followed
closely behind, the sudden uproar was both bewildering and
amusing. His appearance was so convincing that only a few
believed he was a soldier; he could effortlessly blend in as
a local militant. This unique ability became his strength,
enabling him to gather sensitive information while mingling
with the community seamlessly. His natural camouflage also
enhanced his effectiveness in counter-insurgency operations,
where trust and integration were paramount for success.

Back in Shopian, given Aurangzeb's appearance and his
resemblance with the locals, he would often venture out
covertly to get first-hand information about the situation
in the valley and better understand the pulse of the local
population. Aurangzeb had befriended a few locals and created

his own technical database to keep tabs on all surrendered militants, overground workers[26] and other guides in the area. Aurangzeb would often visit this particular tea stall near the company location, which was run by an old lady named Nazeera Begum.

Aurangzeb understood the importance of building trust with the local community, which was more important than just gathering information by cultivating an individual source. He believed that Nazeera Begum, who used to run a tea stall near the company location, could provide valuable insights about the town of Shopian. Every day, people from all walks of life—labourers, traders, etc.—gathered at her stall for their cups of tea, making it a hub of community interaction. Aurangzeb, dressed in an oversized navy blue *phiran*,[27] immersed himself in the local culture, aiming to blend in as a resident. Over time, Nazeera Begum grew fond of his genuine interest and concern. Amidst the bustling activity at her stall, Aurangzeb often found moments to engage in small conversations with her. One day, settling on a wooden bench in front of her stove, he noticed the sadness in Nazeera Begum's eyes. '*Khala, aapki aankhein kaafi dukhi lagti hai. Sab khairiyat?*' (Aunty, your eyes seem pretty sad. Is everything alright?) he gently inquired. Nazeera Begum, usually reserved about her personal life, opened up to Aurangzeb and shared her heart-wrenching story— three years ago, her beloved husband passed away, leaving

---

[26] People who help the militants with logistical support, money and shelter among other things.

[27] A traditional, long, loose-fitted robe designed to keep the body warm, worn by the people of Kashmir as a symbol of their cultural heritage.

behind a daughter who was married off. Her son-in-law, unemployed and addicted to alcohol, subjected her daughter to domestic abuse. '*Samajh he nahi aata kya karein*' (I don't know what to do), she confided in Aurangzeb. Listening intently, Aurangzeb felt a surge of anger and empathy. '*Aapki beti hain Khala. Unhe ghar le aaiye*' (She's your daughter, Aunty. Bring her home), he suggested, his voice tinged with concern. '*Beta, aise nahi hota samaaj mein. Par agar tum uske shauhar ko naukri dilaane mein madad kar pao, toh Allah tumhe barkat dega*' (Son, it's not done like that here. Society has its ways. But if you can help her husband find a job, then Allah will bless you), Nazeera Begum responded, her voice full of hope. Aurangzeb nodded solemnly, understanding the complexities of societal norms and the challenges faced by women like Nazeera Begum. He realized that earning the trust of the locals meant more than just solving problems— it required respecting cultural sensitivities and finding solutions that aligned with the community's values. '*Vaise beta humein pata hai aap fauj mein hain. Mere shauhar bhi informer the fauj ke aur ek atankwadi hamle mein unki jaan chali gayi thi*' (I know you're in Army. My husband worked as a military informer and he lost his life in a militant attack), Nazeera Begum continued wiping her slab and Aurangzeb didn't react. As he left her stall that day, he was determined to find a way to bring a positive change and do everything in his capacity to help Nazeera Begum live a better life; a life without worry at least.

Soon, Aurangzeb managed to convince his Company Commander to get Nazeera Begum's son-in-law a job as a local porter in the nearby Border Road Organisation

Detachment.[28] Over time, her daughter's domestic life became pleasant, and Nazeera Begum was immensely grateful to Aurangzeb. As a goodwill gesture, she introduced him to her nephew Mudassar, who used to work as a carpenter in a local factory. In a matter of days, Mudassar became a trusted companion of Aurangzeb—his source, who would promptly inform him about any suspected militant activities in the area. In military parlance, a source is someone who works for the *tanzeem*;[29] it could either be for the militant organizations or the military personnel. While Informers were individuals who would only pass specific information in return for monetary gains or even liquor, which even today is as valuable as currency in Kashmir.

Aurangzeb taught Mudassar to use WhatsApp to send locations. He would then skilfully mark those locations on maps for effective communication and strategic planning. This one time, Aurangzeb was informed by Mudassar about the movement of militants in Barat Kalan, where foreign militants would occasionally take *panah*[30] in some Haider War's house. He decided to act on the information and painstakingly convinced his Company Commander to allow him to go on the ground to gather first-hand information covertly. He then wore an oversized phiran and asked Mudassar to accompany him to Haider's house. Right in the middle of the village was Haider's abode—a wooden conical modest home with a cowshed outside. Approaching the house, Aurangzeb noticed

[28] A detachment is the dispatch of a body of troops or company away from the main group for a special mission/ additional tasks.

[29] System/organization.

[30] Shelter in Urdu.

the entryway, a humble yet sturdy door made from planks of wood skilfully joined together. Atop the door was a semi-circular lock, weathered by time but still functional, keeping the door latched. Mudassar knocked anxiously on Haider's door, waiting with unease until it creaked open after a few tense seconds. '*Bhaijaan*[31] *bahar hai*' (Brother is out there), Mudassar blurted, portraying Aurangzeb as a foreign terrorist who had crossed into their area and needed shelter for the night. Haider War's face displayed no emotion. 'No,' he said firmly, refusing outright. Mudassar was taken aback—he had been witnessing scenes where militants had entered this very house before. Confusion etched his features as he glanced towards where Aurangzeb was hiding behind the outer wall. Feeling perplexed, Mudassar retreated, unsure of Haider War's adamant refusal. Together, they silently made their way back to their camp. Aurangzeb couldn't join the dots about what led to Haider's refusal. It was indeed a failed attempt but something was amiss.

Aurangzeb went through all the documents the following day and tried to find the missing link. He went through the family's history, and that is when he realized the crucial connection. It wasn't Haider War who worked as an overground worker; it was, in fact, his wife, Rumaiza War. Rumaiza hailed from Anantnag and her brother was a militant who was executed at the hands of the military forces. So, to pay homage to her brother, she enrolled as an overground worker aiding the militants who crossed the border. Such stories were not uncommon in Kashmir at that time. Maybe she hadn't been home when Aurangzeb went,

---

[31] A term of respect for militants used by their sympathizers.

so the husband didn't let them in. The next day, Aurangzeb resolved to return under the cover of darkness. He had learnt that militants had developed subtle methods to notify their overground counterparts of their impending arrival. Some would cut off the electricity supply to a house—a powerful signal that would not go unnoticed in the quiet of night. Others might gently kick the sheep tied outside as the startled bleats of the cattle would echo through the stillness, serving as an auditory cue. Each individual had their own unique way of communicating, ensuring that overground workers remained vigilant and ready. Any unusual movement or activity around them signalled the imminent arrival of militants. This network of signals was crucial for coordination and safety in their operations. Aurangzeb proceeded cautiously, fully aware of the risks and responsibilities that accompanied his role.

Aurangzeb and Mudassar carefully executed their plan by cutting the power supply to Rumaiza War's house, following the militants' protocol to signal their arrival discreetly. Mudassar approached the door while Aurangzeb remained concealed by the side wall. Once again, Haider War opened the door, and upon hearing about the arrival of 'bhaijaan', like the last time, Haider War initially refused. It was then that Rumaiza War emerged from another room, sparking a heated exchange in Kashmiri between husband and wife. After a prolonged debate, Haider War reluctantly allowed Aurangzeb, who was introduced as Jibraan Mohammad, to enter, with Mudassar following suit. In accordance with the militants' standard procedure, upon entering a Kashmiri home, all family members were confined to a single room, their phones confiscated, and their whereabouts and communications restricted. Rumaiza

War, designated as the administrative support, was allowed to step out of the room, and she guided Aurangzeb and Mudassar upstairs to the room on the left.

There, a story was fabricated. Mudassar explained to Rumaiza that 'Jibraan Mohammad' was a foreign terrorist affiliated with Lashkar-e-Taiba, who had crossed over from Pakistan, and soon after crossing the border, the military forces had killed his source. Such radicalized households in Kashmir treated foreign terrorists almost like sacred figures—crusaders who had journeyed from afar in pursuit of their cause. Rumaiza War graciously provided Aurangzeb with a kangri and prepared a delicious meal for both guests. As dawn approached, Aurangzeb, alias Jibraan Mohammad, and Mudassar descended the stairs to depart. During the descent, Aurangzeb noticed a peculiar symbol debossed on the wall—a crescent moon and star between two vertical lines, with 'Allah' inscribed above. Upon inquiry, he learned that Kashmiri women who had lost their family members to military actions displayed such symbols as a mark of commitment to the 'greater cause'. This was new information that had not reached the military circles till now. Impressed by Rumaiza's bravery and dedication, Aurangzeb bid her farewell, promising to return soon. Aurangzeb shared the information he had gathered during his visit with the Company Commander, knowing there was still more to uncover. Under the guise of a militant, he could deceive Rumaiza and gather intelligence on other overground workers operating in the area. Although he had the option to have her detained immediately, he decided to wait, hoping to gather additional valuable insider information before taking further action.

A few days later, Aurangzeb took Mudassar with him to Rumaiza's house to gather more information about other operatives in the area. The night was dark as they walked towards Barat Kalan village, the moonlight casting eerie shadows on the secluded road. Aurangzeb's mind raced with thoughts of the risks ahead and the tension was palpable in the silent air of the night. As they approached Rumaiza's house, something felt off. The usual glow of lights from her home was absent—a clear signal that something was amiss. 'Maybe they're having an electrical malfunction,' Aurangzeb thought to himself as they approached the wooden door. As they reached to knock, Aurangzeb and Mudassar exchanged a glance filled with unspoken concern. They knocked softly, hoping against hope that their fears were unfounded. The door creaked open slowly, revealing Rumaiza's cautious face in the dim light. Rumaiza opened the door and welcomed 'Jibraan Mohammad' inside. Her demeanour seemed different. Normally buzzing with activity, tonight the house seemed unnaturally still. Aurangzeb noticed that all the family members were huddled in one room, which was something they would do upon arrival. Why were they locked in a room? Was there someone else present there? Were 'bhaijaans' under the same roof as Aurangzeb alias Jibraan Mohammad? All sorts of questions and doubts clouded his mind but, of course, Aurangzeb decided to not step back and move ahead with his plan.

However, something didn't add up. Rumaiza guided them upstairs to the room on the right—that in itself rang a bell in Aurangzeb's head as it was contrary to their usual accommodation. '*Aur bhi bhaijaan aaye hue hain*' (there are more 'brothers' here), Rumaiza announced quietly, placing a traditional kangri on the floor. Aurangzeb's heart skipped a beat. The implications of being under the same roof as the militants, potentially outnumbered and outmanoeuvred by them, sent a chill down his spine. His mind raced like a speeding train. What if a military attack happened right there and then? Would his own company label him a traitor because they didn't know where he was? Could this put his family's long-standing reputation at risk? Was there a chance he might be mistaken for a militant pretending to be a soldier all this while in this complicated situation? These thoughts swirled in his head, threatening to show on his face how scared he indeed was. Despite his fear, Aurangzeb tried hard to keep a calm exterior, as if he belonged there. Just then, a formidable figure appeared in the doorway—a man cloaked in a black phiran, his scarf wrapped tightly around his head. A man with a height of 6 feet 2 inches, with a long black beard and eyes that could shake your very core with one stare. He carried an AK-47 with practised ease as his gaze pierced through the room with undeviating intensity. Despite Aurangzeb having a concealed weapon, his nerves were on edge. '*Arey bhaijaan, yeh sarhad paar se aaye hain. Jibraan Mohammad hain inka naam. Lashkar se hain,*' (Brother, they are from across the border. His name is Jibraan Mohammad. He is from Lashkar), Rumaiza explained calmly, her voice displaying no hint of hesitation. Aurangzeb exhaled quietly, grateful that Rumaiza had taken charge of the conversation, sparing him the need to maintain a flawless Pakistani accent that the man with the gun could of course easily detect.

'*Lashkar? Hum bhi Lashkar se hain*' (Lashkar? We are also from Lashkar), the militant declared bluntly, locking eyes with Aurangzeb. Panic surged through Aurangzeb like an electric shock. His mind raced, questioning the odds and regretting every misstep that had brought him to this precarious moment. 'Oh lord! What are the odds? I should have said Jaish-e-Mohammed instead,' he lamented internally, knowing that one wrong move could unravel his carefully constructed façade and blow his cover at any moment. Aurangzeb and Mudassar exchanged tense glances, their eyes darting toward the windows and doorways, searching for any sign of an opportunity to gather crucial intelligence or make an escape. Aurangzeb overheard snippets of conversation—details about four armed militants concealed within the house. It was a breakthrough, vital information that could turn the tide of operations if relayed to his superiors. He knew he had to find the right moment to send an SOS (save our souls) message to the company and mobilize troops to the location. But a sudden, foreboding shadow fell across the room as Aurangzeb's hand moved toward his concealed communication device.

The atmosphere shifted abruptly, thick with an unsettling silence that hinted at imminent danger drawing near. The militant returned towards Aurangzeb, looking suspicious. In that moment, Aurangzeb sensed that his cover was compromised—his training said that any moment your conscience tells you that your cover may have been blown, it already is. The militant advanced, placing his gun against Aurangzeb's forehead, demanding, '*Mukhbir, kaun hai tu?*' (Informant, who are you?) As the militant's finger reached for the trigger, Aurangzeb's training kicked in with razor-sharp precision. In a swift and calculated move, he engaged in hand-to-hand combat, twisting the militant's arm to disarm him.

The room erupted in chaos—there was a flurry of shouts and scrambling movements as Aurangzeb shouted to

Mudassar, '*Khidki se kood! Jao!* (Jump out the window! Go!).
Amid all the chaos and confusion, a sudden gunshot rang out,
grazing Aurangzeb's arm just as he leapt out of the window.
His heart raced as a rush surged through him, making him
hit the ground below. Pain shot through his injured arm, but
he pushed it aside, focusing on what needed to be done to
stay alive. The cold earth met him with an unexpected jolt,
stealing his breath momentarily. Yet, in the urgency of the
moment, there was no time to dwell on the throbbing ache.
Every fibre of his being focused on survival, urging him to
move swiftly and decisively. In the darkness, he could hear
nothing but the echo of that gunshot. His mind raced as he
realized he had to keep moving to get away from the danger
that was closing in. Adrenaline pumped through his veins,
urging him onward. He ran to move as far away from the
house from where he barely managed to escape.

Back at base, Aurangzeb faced a barrage of brickbats from
his stern-faced Company Commander. And why wouldn't he?
This wasn't a *Top Gun* sequel that he ventured into a house
full of armed militants with a concealed weapon and no
backup. The risk he had taken was not appreciated. Despite
the reprimand, Aurangzeb remained deeply committed to
his duty in Shopian, so much so that he even neglected his
personal life in the bargain. It wasn't Aurangzeb's charter to
be making technical surveillance maps or data but it was his
personal choice and maybe his dedication that made him
so well known in the military circle. Aurangzeb had taken
upon himself some sort of a personal mission to weed off
militants from the area. For him, it was his state, his people,
and his country, and he had to do everything in his capacity
to ensure that the next generation woke up to a pleasant

valley. Back home, Ilham would dial Aurangzeb's number quite often, hoping to hear his voice. Days had passed since she last heard him. All she knew from his siblings was that he was on duty, safe and sound. Ilham didn't quite understand the distance. For her, her oxygen was moving away, and she found it increasingly difficult to breathe and navigate life. She felt broken—he had abandoned her while she embraced him as her own. Did she do something to irk him? Had he found his soulmate in someone else? Did he even like her anymore? Ilham's pillow would be soaked with tears every night as her mind felt burdened, as though weighed down by a massive rock of conflicting thoughts pressing upon it.

The more Aurangzeb immersed himself in his duty, the more distant Ilham became from him. Soon, she was like a fading memory in Aurangzeb's story. The distance between them grew, marked by unanswered calls and unopened letters. Aurangzeb had seen children in his village lose their fathers to militant violence; their childhoods snatched by a bullet. He did not want any more brutality or bloodshed in Jammu and Kashmir, so he immersed himself completely in fulfilling his duty as a soldier, even though his own love was hanging by a thread. Surely, Aurangzeb became the soldier he had always dreamed of, but he was no longer the man the girl of his dreams had hoped for. Ilham thought her love story was over, but was it? The man she had imagined her future with was nowhere to be found. Nobody is too busy for love; maybe she didn't matter now. Was this the end even before the beginning?

# #4

# Infiltration

While the Indian Army was busy weeding out militants from Kashmir, the situation grew increasingly tense in Pakistan-occupied Kashmir (PoK). Despite efforts by the Hizbul Mujahideen outfit to destabilize the Kashmir valley, their foothold remained precarious, which was a major roadblock in their cynical ambitions to disrupt the region and sever Kashmir from India. Masood Azhar, a prominent and influential figure within the realm of Islamist militancy, was acutely aware of the strategic impasse and recognized the urgent need for a pivotal figure—someone steadfast and indoctrinated—to instigate unrest and sow seeds of dissent among the local Kashmiri youth. Across the border, in India, development initiatives aimed at bolstering the valley's infrastructure posed a direct challenge to Masood Azhar's disruptive agendas. It was during this critical phase that Abdul Rauf Azhar, Masood Azhar's younger brother, a shadowy figure with ties to the infamous Kandahar hijack of the Indian Airlines flight, proposed a solution—his son, Tallah Rashid. Trained meticulously by Jaish-e-Mohammed operatives over the last several years, Tallah Rashid stood resolute to execute their plans with ruthless efficiency and would also be able to relate with the youth and lure them into their fold.

The year was 1999. Mufti Abdul Rauf Azhar, the operational chief of Jaish-e-Mohammed, a twenty-four-year-old boy, orchestrated an assault where they hijacked the IC-814 Indian Airlines commercial flight on 24 December. The flight was on the route from Tribhuvan International Airport in Kathmandu, Nepal, to Indira Gandhi International Airport in Delhi, India. The hijackers, under the leadership of Abdul Rauf Azhar, worked for nearly six months with one single motive—freedom for the then Harkat-ul-Mujahideen chief Maulana Masood Azhar, who was, at that time, incarcerated in Jammu. Masood Azhar had been infamous for disseminating jihadist propaganda through his writings and audio statements. In 1994, while visiting the Kashmir valley in India on a fake Portuguese passport, he was apprehended by the Indian security forces. Once the hijack took place, after lengthy negotiations that lasted several days, Masood Azhar was freed in exchange for passengers of the Indian Airlines flight. Immediately after his release, Azhar left Harkat-ul-Mujahideen and established Jaish-e-Mohammed in late 2000. Subsequently, Jaish-e-Mohammed was deemed responsible for the attack on the Indian Parliament on 13 December 2001, and the Pulwama attack of 2019 that resulted in the death of forty Indian paramilitary personnel, among many others. Since its inception, the outfit's presence has escalated militant activities in Kashmir, particularly through its involvement in carrying out attacks against Indian security forces and civilian targets. The group is known for its sophisticated tactics, including suicide bombings and *fedayeen*[32] attacks, which have intensified the conflict in the region.

With the coming in of Tallah Rashid, nephew of Masood Azhar, the decade-long aim of destabilizing the Kashmir valley was facing a generational shift. Tallah Rashid was all ready to cross over the border and wreak havoc in the Kashmir valley as he was taught from a very young age. The preparations to clandestinely transfer him across the porous borders were meticulous and swift, orchestrated by their loyal overground workers embedded deep within Kashmiri communities sympathetic to their cause. For Tallah, this covert mission was a defining moment—a crossing of physical borders and a crucial opportunity to uphold and advance a legacy. Each step he took into the Indian territory carried the weight of familial legacy and ideological commitment, which fuelled his resolve and suppressed his apprehensions. Very soon, in the shadowy depths of a moonless night, Tallah crouched low amidst the dense foliage just a stone's throw from the Line of Control (LoC) that separated PoK from the Indian-administered Kashmir. He had slipped through the rugged terrain with a small team of hardened militants, their eyes glinting with eerie determination and fanaticism. Tallah was finally in India.

The air was crisp as the temperature dipped in the higher reaches of Kashmir, where the silence was broken only by the occasional rustle of leaves stirred by the wind. Post the infiltration, Tallah's mind raced with plans to disrupt and indoctrinate the locals. His mission was clear—to sow seeds of dissent and upheaval among the impressionable youth

---

[32] Martyrdom.

of the valley, recruit them into the folds of extremism and execute operations that would destabilize the region. Tallah and his men advanced cautiously and stealthily towards their designated rendezvous point as each member was attuned to the dangers of detection by Indian border patrols. En route to their safe house, Tallah's thoughts drifted to the training sessions back in Muzaffarabad, where his commander had drilled in them lessons on insurgency and psychological warfare tactics. He recalled the fiery speeches that his uncle delivered, stoking their fervour for jihad and martyrdom. A faint glimmer of anticipation flickered in Tallah's eyes as they neared a makeshift, secluded hut in the wilderness that was to be their temporary base of operations in Kashmir—a clandestine hub for planning and coordination. It was a Jaish-e-Mohammed safe house. Inside, the air was thick with the scent of damp earth and the tang of gunpowder. Crude maps of the Kashmir valley adorned the walls, marked with strategic targets and potential recruits. A wooden table stood at the centre, surrounded by mismatched chairs worn smooth by years of use. The floorboards creaked underfoot which showed the condition of the hut. The room whispered with memories of hushed conversations and radio transmissions, a space where secrets could find a home. A rusty kerosene lantern rested on the rickety shelf, its glass globe clouded with dust and spiderwebs, but still functional, casting a flicking glow that added to the aura of the covert mission. The silence within was profound, broken only by the occasional rustle of the wind through the trees or the distant cry of a bird—Tallah found it to be the perfect place to regroup and strategize before merging with the local populace of Kashmir. He gathered his men around the flickering lantern and spoke with conviction, his voice low yet commanding, outlining the tasks ahead. Plans were discussed in hushed tones, outlining propaganda campaigns to exploit grievances among the local populace and schemes to recruit disaffected youth disillusioned with the status quo. With the plan set, Tallah's mind raced with the enormity of the task before him—to harness the simmering discontent and channel it into acts of insurgency that would shake the very foundation of Kashmir's stability. Days blurred into nights as Tallah and his cohorts moved like phantoms through the valleys and villages of Kashmir. They met with local sympathizers, weaving tales of sacrifice and martyrdom, and enticing the vulnerable with promises of glory and a cause greater than themselves. In the weeks that followed, sporadic acts of violence erupted across the valley—bombings, ambushes and targeted assassinations— all orchestrated by Tallah's network of operatives. His brutal forces made the streets across the valley echo with the wails of sirens and the distant crackle of gunfire.

Back in Aurangzeb's unit, sometime around the end of August 2017, an Intelligence Bureau agent visited. He informed the officer that a report had arrived where a few militants had crossed the line of control a few weeks ago and might be heading towards Pulwama. Their exact locations and identities were yet to be discovered. It was suspected that the recent surge in militant activities around the valley was a result of the disruptive activities of these men. Though Tallah Rashid remained elusive through it all, he was a shadowy figure lurking in the periphery of Kashmir's turbulent landscape. As the seasons changed and the valley started preparing for the impending winter, Tallah continued his unabated mission, a grim harbinger of unrest amidst Kashmir's snow-capped peaks and verdant valleys.

Over time, Tallah had successfully recruited several
local youths from the valley, the most notable being Wasim
Ahmed Ganie—a class tenth dropout from Beerwah Village
in the Tral Area of Jammu and Kashmir. The son of a poultry
farmer, Wasim had accompanied his childhood friend to
Rathsuna village, which was not that far, to attend the funeral
of Hizbul Mujahideen Commander Sabzar Ahmad Bhat, a
close ally of Burhan Wani.[33] That day, Rathsuna village had
come alive with songs about jihad echoing through the dusty,
crowded streets, where mourners had gathered to pay their
last respects. In their eyes, they had lost a warrior, a crusader
fighting for their freedom. While most men gathered around
Sabzar Ahmad Bhat's lifeless body, others struggled to get a
glimpse of Bhat for one last time. Boys on motorbikes and
taxis, waving green flags, reached the village. Soon, anti-India
slogans filled the air. 'Hum kya chahte?—Azaadi!' (What do we
want?—Freedom!), they chanted in unison, with voices that
were raw with anguish and anger. Meanwhile, the atmosphere
in the village grew increasingly charged with emotion. Some
mourners threw stones towards the distant silhouette of an
armoured vehicle as a symbolic gesture of their resistance.
As Wasim listened to the impassioned speeches and fervent
chants of 'Azaadi', he felt a surge of emotions stir within
him. After paying their last respects, when the crowd began
to disperse, Wasim lingered near Sabzar Ahmad Bhat's grave,
his heart heavy with a newfound sense of purpose. He felt
liberated as though he had found his calling. He picked up
a discarded banner emblazoned with the words, 'Freedom

---

[33] A commander of Hizbul Mujahideen who soon became the poster boy
of militancy in Kashmir. He was executed by the military forces in 2016.

for Kashmir', clutched it tightly in his hands and smiled as
though his own feelings were painted on the tattered white
cloth. As he made his way home, Wasim's thoughts raced
with possibilities. He imagined himself joining the ranks
of those who, according to him, dared to raise their voice
against the men in uniform. He was somewhat moved by the
stories of the supposed atrocities inflicted on the locals, and
agreed that they could only progress through the sword of
liberation. That night, Wasim lay awake in his modest room,
where the trembling light of a kerosene lamp cast shadows of
the banner on the wall. He traced the contours of the banner
in his hands, engraving every alphabet in his memory. At that
moment, Wasim knew that he had taken his first step down
a path that would test his courage, challenge his convictions
and bind him to a struggle that had shaped the destiny of
Kashmir for generations. Unable to ignore the call to action
that pulsed through his veins, Wasim decided to alter the
course of his life forever.

One chilly evening, as the sun slipped below the horizon
and shadows lengthened across the streets of Beerwah village,
Wasim quietly slipped away from his house. With a few meagre
belongings hastily packed in a tattered backpack, he navigated
the familiar route with a sense of purpose that overshadowed
his fear. He knew the risk of his decision—the potential
repercussions for his family, the danger of violence that lurked
around every corner—but he was driven by an unflinching
belief in the so-called righteousness of his cause. Guided by
a network of sympathizers, Wasim ventured deeper into the
rugged terrain of the Kashmir countryside. The landscape,
illuminated by the silver glow of the moonlight, seemed to
guide him forward—a silent witness to the aspirations and

dreams of generations past and present. Boys like Wasim were quite a lot in Kashmir, who would get swayed by a few words of a world far away. After Wasim made the impulsive decision to leave home and join the militants, his journey took unexpected twists and turns that ultimately led him into the fold of Tallah Rashid's militant group. They were looking for young boys like Wasim and here, he had landed straight into their lap. After weeks of training and integration into a smaller cell within the insurgency, Wasim's reputation grew as a committed and skilled recruit. He proved himself in skirmishes against the Indian security forces, demonstrating both bravery and tactical understanding beyond his years. His *josh*[34] for the cause and his dedication caught the attention of Tallah Rashid himself.

Tallah, having heard of Wasim's exploits and sensing potential in the young recruit, personally sought him out during a covert meeting in a remote mountain pass. Tallah's steely gaze and aura of authority left an indelible mark on Wasim—he had found his role model. Tallah had been orchestrating a big blow in Kashmir, the planning of which started a few months ago. He knew that being a young boy and a native, Wasim would be a huge asset in his aim to destabilize the valley, an aspiration that was camouflaged to project that he was fighting for the rights of the people of Kashmir. Impressed by Wasim's enthusiasm and potential, Tallah offered him a pivotal role within his inner circle—he was tasked with coordinating logistics for covert operations and ensuring the smooth execution of missions ranging from ambushes on military convoys to propaganda campaigns

---

[34] Zeal.

aimed at galvanizing public support. Under Tallah's mentorship, Wasim's skills developed rapidly. He learned the art of persuasion and recruitment, adeptly swaying disillusioned youth and villagers to join their cause. As weeks passed, Wasim became an integral part of Tallah Rashid's operations. He earned the respect of his comrades through the courage displayed on the ground and his unwavering commitment to their shared ideals. Together with Tallah and the other militants, Wasim traversed the rugged terrain of Kashmir, evading security sweeps and striking targets with precision and stealth. As Wasim stood alongside Tallah Rashid, overlooking the mist-shrouded valleys of Kashmir, he knew that he had found his place in history—a reluctant student turned fervent advocate for a cause greater than himself. He was so indoctrinated by the dreamy words of Tallah Rashid that Wasim remained determined in his belief that, one day, Kashmir would be free. Wasim made his place and felt a sense of belonging with Tallah Rashid. He was then introduced to Tallah's dream plan for which Masood Azhar had sent him to India. Tallah Rashid had marked his target, an attack so profound that it would echo for years to come.

Ghulam Hassan Geelani was a wealthy, reputed businessman in the valley, who was also very well-connected with the top political brass of the country. The militants had been circling his name for quite a while. It was decided that they would plan something for 12 December, the date when Geelani's son's *walima*[35] was scheduled. It would be the event of the decade for Kashmir, a gathering so grand that it had been the talk of the town for months now. Tallah Rashid knew that

---

[35] Wedding reception.

Geelani's ancestral home in Batmaloo, Srinagar would be the epicentre where the who's who of the valley would converge under one roof to celebrate his son's wedding. Not just that, looking at the security arrangements that had been rehearsed since June 2017, it became evident that a few political leaders would be travelling from New Delhi to bless the newlywed couple. Tallah Rashid knew that if he could covertly enter the venue and blow it into pieces, his name would be written in golden ink on the pages of jihad, and he would have a special place reserved for him in *jannat*.[36]

---

[36] Heaven.

hope amidst the uncertainty that hung in the air. While she rested, her husband was out getting medicine from a local store as prescribed by the doctor. At the heart of the clinic was the doctor—a stalwart figure with greying hair and compassionate eyes who moved with practised efficiency, tending to his patients with care and compassion.

It was then that Tallah Rashid and Wasim barged into the clinic with their hands gripping their respective weapons. Before the doctor could even speak, Tallah gestured for silence, his gaze intense yet controlled. He conveyed their situation with a glance—time was running short, and their lives depended on the doctor's discretion. But, it wasn't like the doctor had a choice of refusal—Tallah had a weapon.

As the military's presence loomed, the clinic became an unlikely safe house for Tallah and Wasim. They huddled in the cramped confines of a storage room where the shelves were laden with boxes of medical supplies and faded linens. The air was thick with the mingling scents of herbs and antiseptic. Outside, the village began to stir with the approaching rumble of military vehicles and the measured footsteps of soldiers coming through the alleyways. While one party had cordoned off the entire village with all exit points blocked, the other group of soldiers approached the village centre. Tallah Rashid pressed his ear against the thin wall, straining to discern the movements outside. The urgency of their situation was palpable as their concealment in the clinic was a fragile hideout, it wasn't the best solution but it was the only one in the current scenario. However, there were greater chances of a face-off as the clinic was on the main road of the village and the cordon and search operation would have commenced any moment. As the military operation intensified, the initial cordon was tightened, sealing off all escape routes and limiting the movement of people within the village. Soldiers of 44 RR, now reinforced by a platoon of J&K Police, swept through the narrow lanes and alleyways with methodical precision, their presence announced by the rumble of vehicles and the authoritative crackle of radio transmissions. In the middle of the escalating tension, an authoritative voice boomed over the loudspeaker. It was that of the Aurangzeb's Company Commander. The announcement echoed through the quiet streets, compelling villagers to emerge from their homes and gather in the open ground of the government school. This was a protocol that the military followed. In any mission, before the soldiers would commence door-to-door search operations, the villagers would be gathered in an open space to verify their identities. In response to the call, the villagers who had earlier escaped to their homes at the first visual of military vehicles hesitantly emerged from their homes, casting wary glances at the armed soldiers who stood watchful and vigilant. Families gathered in clusters, children clutching their parents' hands, elders leaning on canes for support. After repeated announcements, the village soon converged on the ground. Their identities were then verified and humane interrogation techniques, as per the laid down norms, were undertaken. Soldiers armed with rifles and accompanied by specially trained search dogs began the laborious task of conducting house-to-house searches. Aurangzeb's party started searching the village from its right flank, where the clinic was. His team cautiously approached each dwelling, their movements deliberate and coordinated to minimize risks and maximize efficiency. With a rifle held with a blend of readiness and restraint, clad in camouflage fatigue and a helmet with a bulletproof jacket hugging his chest, Aurangzeb moved from one house to the other, meticulously searching through all doors and godowns. Advanced surveillance equipment, including thermal imaging cameras and handheld metal detectors, supplemented the soldiers' efforts to detect hidden compartments or concealed weapons. Every house, including the livestock pens, was searched with meticulous thoroughness to find the wanted militants.

Just as Aurangzeb was on with the search operation, he heard a loud wail of a woman—a cry so profound that it shattered the uneasy quiet. Aurangzeb paused mid-stride, his eyes focused and zeroed in on the source of the cries. Though the clinic's elderly patient and the child complied quietly when the soldier first ordered the villagers to step out, the doctor didn't want to abandon his patient and continued tending to the pregnant woman. The woman lay on a simple cot, her face contorted with anguish as labour pains gripped her abdomen. Inside the clinic, the doctor's forehead creased with concern as he moved about with urgency preparing for the imminent birth right in the middle of a military operation. Just then, the woman's wails were supplanted by the distant cry of a man—dressed in a mud-brown Pathani suit running in the direction of the clinic with frantic urgency.

'Please, my wife!' he pleaded, his voice cracking with emotion. 'She's in labour; she needs me!' The soldier intercepted the man as the area was unsafe to venture into. Amidst this tableau of anguish and authority, Aurangzeb, who was carrying out the search operation, stood still with the rifle clutched in his steady hands. He was trying to decipher the source of the wail and was also cautious of the fact that it could be a decoy. The cries intensified with every passing moment and it struck a chord of urgency within Aurangzeb, igniting a swift and resolute response born of both duty and empathy. In a decisive moment, Aurangzeb closed the distance between himself and the clinic while being vigilant.

Inside the clinic, Tallah Rashid's heart sank as he heard the commotion outside. The approaching footsteps of the soldiers reverberating through the walls were like a drumbeat of impending danger. He knew their precarious hiding place could not remain concealed for long if the woman's agonizing cries continued to echo. And so, Tallah Rashid peeped through the rust-coloured curtain and gestured the doctor not to make any sound. Unfortunately for him, the force of nature was far more robust than the command of the militant. Beads of sweat traced a slow, hesitant descent down his temples following a path that mirrored the uncertainty that gripped his conflicting mind. Tallah looked in all directions hurriedly—he just couldn't think. As Aurangzeb drew nearer, his footsteps measured and purposeful, the intensity of Tallah's internal struggle grew palpable. The rhythmic cadence of the approaching soldier, amplified by the pregnant woman's cries, pierced through the stillness with unrestrained urgency and posed as a haunting backdrop to Tallah's inner turmoil. Each heartbeat of his echoed in sync with Aurangzeb's advance, and every step heightened the stakes of their unfolding confrontation. For a second, Tallah thought, he was marooned in the clinic with no solution in sight.

In a heartbeat, the pregnant woman's cries reached a crescendo as she clutched onto the sky-blue bedspread. Tallah Rashid couldn't take it any more. With the peak in her cries, his rage skyrocketed. He immediately looked towards his rifle as his hands closed around the familiar weight of his weapon. In a flash, the direction of the muzzle shifted from the entryway of the clinic onto the pregnant lady. Tallah's gaze locked onto the woman with a mix of anger and resolve. In a tragic twist of fate, just as Aurangzeb was a few steps away from the clinic, Tallah Rashid's decision was made. His finger tightened on the trigger and with the deafening crack of the gunfire, the wails were no longer heard. The pregnant woman's cries ceased abruptly and were replaced by the stunned silence that hung heavy in the air. Outside, Aurangzeb's steady advance faltered, his footsteps receded as he recognized the target of the bullet. The tragic gunshot silenced everything outside in an instant. The soldiers approaching the clinic took cover as silence filled the air, but they knew that it was the quiet before the storm.

That day, the clinic walls in Aglar Kandi bore witness to an atrocity so grave that no word could justify it. With bullets raining, the doctor lay in a pool of blood with a gauze sponge in one hand and a medical injection in the other. What was more gruesome was that Tallah Rashid's bullet had killed two heartbeats in a single shot—the child was killed with its mother before it could even open its eyes to the world. As he sat with his back against the rough-hewn wall of the clinic, Wasim saw Tallah Rashid wreak havoc in the four walls of the clinic. In profound disbelief, he couldn't speak once he saw the events unfold before him. Wasim's forehead creased as he replayed the scenes in his mind—villagers caught in the crossfire, the pregnant woman's tragic fate and the ruthless decisions made in the name of liberation. 'Was this the struggle he was fighting for?' Wasim wondered. The ideals of freedom and justice, once so fervently espoused by Tallah and his comrades, now seemed tarnished by the harsh reality of their methods. Wasim had joined the cause with dreams of a better future for Kashmir, but now he found himself grappling with doubts that gnawed at the edges of his commitment. 'Was it worth it?' The question echoed in his mind. The sacrifices demanded by their struggle— of lives lost and futures ruined—now seemed too steep for Wasim. Glancing around the dimly lit room, his eyes settled on Tallah Rashid, whose commanding presence had once inspired loyalty and admiration. Now, all he could see was a figure consumed by a relentless pursuit of power, blind to the human cost exacted along the way. 'Was Tallah actually a well-wisher?' The doubt crept in like tendrils of smoke, obscuring the clarity of purpose that had once guided Wasim's every action. The dichotomy of a leader who professed liberation yet sanctioned the deaths of his own people weighed heavily on his conscience.

'How can one be on the right path if it involves killing your own people?' The question hung in the air, posing a moral dilemma in Wasim's already troubled mind. His conflicted thoughts compelled him to edge closer to the clinic entrance. Sensing Wasim's movement, Tallah had to act swiftly. Owing to the imminent danger of discovery, Tallah had no recourse but to silence Wasim with a decisive gunshot. At that moment, a boy all of fifteen, who had big dreams for Kashmir and its people, lay lifeless on the wooden floor of the clinic. His only fault was that he trusted the wrong people in his desperation to secure a better life. After the gunshot, the soldiers surrounding the clinic tightened their grip, their commands for surrender resounded through the tense air, marking the beginning of a critical stand-off. Tallah Rashid, observing the movement outside, remained surprisingly optimistic. He knew that if he could manage to escape the cordon, their plan of attacking Srinagar could still fructify, as he had time to activate a new set of disenfranchised youth. Standing in a room that looked no less than a battlefield with three lifeless people lying around and blood scattered all over, Tallah started looking for a place to escape while occasionally firing through the corners of the windows. Aurangzeb's company, though involved in counter-retaliatory fire, couldn't blow up the clinic as they weren't sure of the number of civilians trapped or held hostage by the militants. Inside the four walls, Tallah's breath came in ragged gasps as he continued looking for escape routes. With each turn, he felt the walls closing in, the weight of his actions pressing down upon him like a suffocating cloak. As Tallah Rashid darted past the storage room, his eyes caught site of an old, weathered stairway tucked in the background. Without hesitation, he sprinted towards it as the wooden planks creaked faintly under his hurried footsteps. The stairs seemed to stretch endlessly upward and each ascent brought him closer to the possibility of escape. Reaching the top, Tallah pushed open a heavy, rusted door that led onto the clinic's rooftop terrace. A few hours had passed since the operation commenced, and the light of the sun's golden hour spilled across the uneven wooden planks placed on one side of the terrace. As he calculated his next move, adrenaline surged through Tallah's veins like a torrential river. Halfway out the door, Tallah paused momentarily, scanning the rooftops of nearby houses looming in the distance. The chasm between them seemed narrow and manageable, offering a precarious route towards potential freedom. The clinic was cordoned off from all sides, surrounded by soldiers closing in like a tightening noose. Even though the rooftops presented a slim chance, it was an opportunity that Tallah couldn't afford to ignore. With resolute hardening in his gaze, he took a deep breath and climbed on top of the roof. Each leap was a calculated risk, and every landing was a test of balance and agility. Time seemed to stretch and compress simultaneously with moments blurring into one another as Tallah Rashid vaulted from roof to roof. His pulse thundered in his ears, drowning out the chaos below.

A sudden shout from below jolted Tallah from his unstable rhythm. He glanced over his shoulder, catching a glimpse of soldiers scrambling onto the roofs behind him. Panic surged anew, urging him to push harder; his lungs burnt with exertion as he darted and dodged amid the rain of bullets. Each impact of a stray shot against the stone walls sent shivers down his spine, a visceral reminder of the danger that was closing in from all sides. Fear clawed at Tallah's chest as he navigated the gaps between rooftops with the soldiers following suit. His body strained with the effort to maintain balance amid the dizzying heights. His fingers clenched around the grip of his weapon. Each shot he fired was a desperate plea for freedom—a calculated risk in the deadly game of cat and mouse unfolding above the quiet village. But as he neared the edge of the last hut, dread settled like a stone in Tallah's gut. The distance to the next rooftop was insurmountable—a gaping chasm that mocked his fleeting hopes of escape. There was nowhere left to go. With the soldiers closing in on him, Tallah breathed heavily as he realized that the chase was over; his hope to escape was shattered. He had taken the risk of penetrating India from under the fence, and he couldn't give up easily.

He looked on all sides and found an escape—a rusty sewage pipe at the edge of the rooftop, snaking down towards the ground. Without batting an eye, Tallah gripped the cold metal. Sliding down with reckless abandon, he hit the ground with a jarring thud and mud splattering around him. Pain shot through his limbs as he landed, but he pushed through, driven by the urgency of survival. What he hadn't realized was that all this while, he had been navigating the treacherous terrain under the watchful eyes of Aurangzeb, who was mirroring his movements on the ground. The weight of responsibility bore down heavily on Aurangzeb's shoulders— Tallah's capture meant safeguarding Kashmir's fragile peace, while his escape threatened to unravel it all. Aurangzeb's finger tightened around his weapon as he sprinted the streets to prevent catastrophe.

Fate seemed to conspire against Tallah Rashid. The sewage pipe had brought him to the ground, away from immediate danger, or so he thought. For him, he had tricked the Indian Army soldiers, the thought of which sent arrogance, against the gravity, to his head. With a fleeting smirk of achievement tugging at the corners of his lips, Tallah ran through the village's twisty streets, his footsteps thudding loudly in the deserted lanes. The narrow alleys blurred past him; each turn was a calculated gamble in his desperate bid for freedom. As he navigated the lanes, the golden hour bathed the village in a soft, amber glow, casting long shadows that stretched across the cobblestone alleys. In the quiet evening, Tallah struggled with the turmoil in his heart as he held onto the hope of outrunning the soldiers who were chasing him relentlessly. Just when he thought freedom was near and he rounded a sharp curve, the golden hue of the evening painted Aurangzeb's figure at the end of the narrow alleyway. The seasoned soldier stood strong-willed, his presence formidable against the backdrop of fading daylight.

Tallah's pace faltered as the smirk of triumph melted away into a knot of dread and terror. Time seemed to slow to a crawl as he and Aurangzeb locked eyes; a moment suspended in time that bridged the distance between the hunter and the hunted. The passage seemed to shrink around them with shadows closing in like spectres of fate. It was an unspoken clash of emotions passing between them in the haunting silence. Aurangzeb's gaze was steady, piercing through Tallah's bravado. Just then, Aurangzeb had an epiphany—the man standing before him, locked in this tense stand-off, was none other than the elusive Tallah Rashid, an A++ category militant with extensive links across the border. The biggest impediment that the military faced in safeguarding the lives of innocent civilians, this man had been a photograph in intelligence briefings all this while and now he stood before Aurangzeb. This realization sharpened his determination to bring an end to Tallah's reign of terror once and for all. As Aurangzeb steadied himself, his grip tightening on his weapon, he knew that this moment held profound implications. In the coming moments, Aurangzeb knew that decisions would be made and consequences faced as the fragile peace of the valley was balanced on a knife's edge.

Tallah Rashid's eyes bulged and muscles coiled like a spring ready to launch into a desperate sprint. But Aurangzeb's presence was an immovable barrier; a stark reminder that there was no escape from the consequences of his choices. Even then, in a daring step born of desperation, Tallah raised his hands in a gesture to surrender—a calculated move to deceive his adversary. As Aurangzeb moved closer, anticipation thickened the air. With a sudden burst of energy, Tallah lunged forward and pushed Aurangzeb's chest with all his might. Aurangzeb staggered back, as though caught off guard by Tallah's audacity.

Before he could even react, Tallah sprinted past him, his feet pounding against the cobblestones as he ran towards the village periphery. Just then, Aurangzeb's voice pierced the air behind him, a mix of frustration and resolve: '*Tallah! Ruk! Tera khel khatam hai*' (Tallah, stop! Your game is over.) As Tallah glanced back, his feet pivoting away from Aurangzeb, Aurangzeb's finger coiled on the trigger. The crack of gunfire followed by bullets tore through the air with deadly precision, sealing Tallah Rashid's fate in an instant. Pain exploded through Tallah's body as he stumbled forward—every step was a battle against physical agony. Aurangzeb didn't stop. For every innocent life lost, for the wailing pregnant woman, for all the atrocities inflicted by Tallah Rashid, Aurangzeb kept harassing the trigger. With a ragged breath, every step that Tallah Rashid took was a war against the darkness that was closing in around him. The village streets blurred past him in a whirling of shadows and pain. Blood soaked through his clothes; a grim reminder of the wounds that marked his body. As his strength ebbed and darkness closed in, Tallah's thoughts turned inward—spiralling amidst the pandemonium of what-ifs and could-have-been. As he crumpled to the ground, the world around Tallah Rashid faded into oblivion. The alleyway fell silent once again as he lay motionless where he had fallen. His tragic end was a reminder of the tangled web that cloisters you on the path of violence and how the route of destruction culminates at such an inglorious end.

Aurangzeb knew all too well that the death of one militant could never compensate for the innocent lives lost— the pregnant woman and the unborn child killed by Tallah Rashid, the children whose laughter had been silenced too soon. Their faces haunted his thoughts as he saw the human cost of the relentless struggle against insurgency and terror. Yet, amid the sad aftermath, Aurangzeb felt a sense of grim satisfaction, a solemn acknowledgement that justice had been served, albeit in the most irreversible ways. As his steps moved away from the lane where Tallah Rashid had met his end, a tornado of emotions crashed over him. The bustling village lanes, now shrouded in the soft glow of dusk, lay eerily quiet—a stark contrast to the chaos that had just unfolded. The air was heavy with the lingering scent of gunpowder and the palpable weight of grief. The golden light of dusk cast long shadows over the cobblestone alleys, where crimson stains marked the places where lives had been shattered. Aurangzeb's eyes swept over the scene, taking in the sad faces of villagers who had gathered with expectant eyes, waiting for reassurance that they could finally return to their homes.

Soldiers moved with purpose around him, some recovering weapons while others tending to the wounded against the backdrop of the village frozen in the aftermath of violence. Aurangzeb's steps led him inevitably towards the epicentre of the battle—the clinic, a place now transformed into a scene of sorrow. The earth beneath his feet seemed to tremble with sorrow as he crossed the entrance threshold into the clinic. Inside, the scene unfolded before him with devastating clarity. Blood had stained the walls in cruel splatters, a view that was an unfortunate reminder of the chaotic struggle that had unfolded within these once-peaceful, healing walls. The lifeless body of a young boy lay near the entryway with his fingers outstretched. The bloodstained doorknob made it apparent the boy must have tried to escape the carnage that engulfed him before being shot; a futile attempt indeed. An old doctor lay slumped against the wall, his glasses askew and a stethoscope dangling limply from his neck—a silent casualty of the senseless violence that had shattered the sanctity of his healing oasis.

In the haunting stillness, the sight that made Aurangzeb's heart constrict with anguish was the crumpled form of a nine-month-pregnant woman, her once vibrant dress now a canvas of tragedy—stained with the crimson of her own lifeblood. Beside her, her husband knelt on the cold, wooden floor, his face a mask of devastation and disbelief. His hands trembled as they moved over her still belly, unable to comprehend the tragedy that had befallen them. The husband's face was a mosaic of agony and denial, etched with lines of despair that spoke of dreams that were shattered in a heartbeat. His eyes, which were otherwise bright with anticipation of upcoming fatherhood, now mirrored the depths of his grief as they stared absently at his lifeless wife and child that couldn't see the light of day. His fingers grazed the delicate swell of her abdomen, an otherwise gesture of love and longing that was now met with silence and emptiness. Aurangzeb felt a lump rise in his throat as his eyes stung with unshed tears. The devastation before him was overwhelming—a cruel reminder of the innocent lives lost in the crossfire of conflict. He clenched his fists, anger coursing through him at the unmitigated brutality that had shattered the peace of Aglar Kandi. The young woman's face, once filled with hopeful excitement as she was about to unveil a beautiful chapter of her life, now appeared still, contrary to how brutal her death was. Her eyes, now motionless, seemed to hold dreams of a life that was abruptly ended by the militants. Standing by the bedside, Aurangzeb could feel the husband's deep sadness, as his occasional sobs pierced the heavy silence in the room. The man uttered broken words of love and loss, his voice cracking with the weight of unspoken sorrow. Aurangzeb stood there silently as his own heart was heavy with the burden of witnessing such profound brutality and loss.

Outside, the villagers waited anxiously, their eyes searching for answers amid the wreckage of their shattered lives. Aurangzeb knew that the scars of this day would run deep as a painful reminder of the fragility of life and the indiscriminate nature of violence. As he looked upon the devastation wrought by Tallah Rashid's insurgency, he made a silent vow—the senseless tragedy would not be forgotten; justice would be sought, not just for the fallen woman and her unborn child, but for all those who had perished in the mindful act of brutality.

As he hurried to leave the clinic, Aurangzeb cast a final glance at the young husband. Their eyes met briefly, exchanging a silent understanding of shared heartache. Aurangzeb felt guilty; he thought that if he had responded a little faster, the woman could now be welcoming a child. With hesitant steps and a heavy heart, he returned to his company location. Behind him, the clinic stood like a silent witness to the horrors—its walls now bore tales of suffering for a husband robbed of his beloved wife and unborn child.

\* \* \*

*In the Tallah Rashid encounter, India lost a brave soldier whose identity remains unknown for security reasons. Yet, his selfless courage and dedication to duty speak volumes, reminding us of the sacrifices made by countless heroes. Though his name may not be spoken, his memory lives on in the hearts of a nation grateful for his unwavering service and sacrifice. Today, we bow our heads in solemn tribute, honouring this unnamed hero for his extraordinary bravery in defence of our land and liberty.*

\* \* \*

# #6

# Human Behind the Camouflage

As days passed after the operation that ended with the death of Tallah Rashid, Aurangzeb found himself immersed in the routine of military life. The company headquarters buzzed with the usual activities—intelligence reports flowing, patrols setting out, frequent operations, preparations for upcoming missions and the meticulous planning that defined their responsibilities in the volatile region. Yet, amidst the outward semblance of normalcy, a storm was brewing within Aurangzeb's heart and mind. The memory of the clinic haunted him like a restless spirit, refusing to fade with time. Each day felt like a continuous replay of the tragic events that had unfolded—the bloodstained walls, the lifeless body of the pregnant woman, the inconsolable grief etched on her husband's face. Aurangzeb carried the weight of those images with him; a burden that grew heavier with each passing night. Nights were the worst. Aurangzeb would often wake up gasping for air, his head pounding with the resounding voices of the woman's cries and howls of anguish that had pierced the silence on that fateful day. Sleep became a fleeting refuge. Nightmares plagued his sleep as he would often wake up with cold sweats. Aurangzeb found himself increasingly withdrawn. The bloodstains may have faded from the streets of Aglar Kandi village but their memory would haunt Aurangzeb as though it happened just yesterday.

One evening, as Aurangzeb sat in the barracks, he found himself unable to shake off the suffocating sense of guilt and helplessness. Even his comrades noticed the change in him. The once cheerful and composed soldier was now plagued by moments of silent introspection and distant stares.

The following day, during a routine briefing session, Aurangzeb's detachment didn't go unnoticed by the Company Commander. A seasoned officer with years of experience in the field, the Company Commander recognized the signs of emotional strain that often accompanied such harrowing missions. As soldiers filed into the briefing room, exchanging nods and quiet greetings, the atmosphere became heavy with anticipation for the day's operational plans. Aurangzeb, usually composed and focused, appeared distracted. His eyes, ordinarily alert, now held a distant, haunting look.

Throughout the briefing, his responses were curt and detached. His usually steady voice faltered slightly as the Company Commander asked him for a report of their recent activities and the status of ongoing operations. Sensing Aurangzeb's inner turmoil in the subtle tremor of his hands as he moved the pointer on the map, the commander decided to address the situation. After dismissing others from the briefing room, he motioned for Aurangzeb to remain. The air seemed charged with unspoken tension as the two men stood facing each other, the weight of unspoken words hanging heavy between them. 'Aurangzeb,' the Company Commander began, his voice a blend of authority and genuine concern. '*Tum kaafi alag lag rahe ho Tallah Rashid wale incident ke baad se. Kuch toh hai jo tumhe pareshan kar raha hai.*' (I've noticed a change in you since the Tallah Rashid operation. It's clear that something's weighing on your mind.) As he spoke, the company commander directed Aurangzeb to occupy the black chair in front of them. Aurangzeb nodded silently. His own eyes reflected a blend of gratitude towards the Company Commander, yet also revealed reluctance to acknowledge the turmoil within him. He felt a lump form in his throat as the floodgates of suppressed emotions threatened to burst open. '*Tum akele nahi ho*' (You're not alone in this), the Company Commander continued, his tone softening with empathy. '*Aise operation mein kayi ghav aise hote hain jo dikhte nahin hain. Tumne jo clinic mein dekha voh koi sadharan mission nahi tha. Woh insaaniyat ka anth tha. Par usme tumhari koi galti nahi thi. Khud ko zimmedar thehrana band karo*' (War leaves scars that aren't always visible. What you witnessed in the clinic—it wasn't just another mission. It was a tragedy that cut to the core of our humanity. But let's make one thing clear: it wasn't your fault. So, stop blaming yourself for what happened). Aurangzeb met the Company Commander's gaze and found solace in the understanding that it reflected. '*Kuch din chutti lo, apne aap ko sambhalo. Tum humare best soldier mein se ek ho. Isko mera order samajhna*' (Take a few days off. Clear your mind, find your balance again. We need you at your best and that means taking care of yourself first. Treat this as a direct order, soldier), the company commander said firmly, yet with a compassion that softened his authority.

Gratitude welled up within Aurangzeb as he nodded in silent acquiescence. The Company Commander's words offered a lifeline—a chance to confront the demons that haunted his nights and find a way to balance the soldier's duty with the emotional toll it demanded from his soul.

Aurangzeb rose from his chair, saluted the officer and moved out. As his steps proceeded towards his barracks, the words of the Company Commander echoed in Aurangzeb's mind, offering a lifeboat amid the stormy sea of conflicting emotions.

For Aurangzeb, putting on his uniform meant more than just a job; it was a sacred promise that symbolized his dedication to defending India's dignity and ensuring the welfare of its people. It meant prioritizing others before himself and standing shoulder to shoulder with his comrades against any danger that threatened their nation. But in the aftermath of the Tallah Rashid operation, the line between duty and the cost to humanity had blurred into a haunting reality. For Aurangzeb, the camouflage fatigues, a symbol of pride and honour, were witness to the barbarity. Each insignia, and every fold and wrinkle seemed to whisper a solemn prayer for the lives lost. Aurangzeb may have been donning his camouflage fatigues, honouring his commitment as a soldier, but deep within his heart, he bled for the innocent.

In the dimly lit, dusty barracks, filled with the familiar scent of military-issue equipment, Aurangzeb methodically folded his uniform and packed his belongings. The anticipation of a leave that usually brought joy was now mingled with apprehension. He couldn't recall the last time he had been home. And Ilham—months had passed since he last spoke to her. He felt guilty, but his love for her hadn't diminished since the day they parted ways. But did she feel the same for him? He wasn't sure if he was in the right frame of mind to face her. He worried about being seen as vulnerable and broken, especially since she might expect him to approach her and fix her broken heart. It was unfortunate that as he headed home after months away, he carried the haunting weight of the last operation with him.

While packing, each item—a worn-out photo of his parents, a birthday card made by Shazia, his little sister, and a small Quran—held profound significance. They were his anchors in a world beyond the battlefield; a reminder of the love and support that awaited him at home in Salani. Ammi's warm smile and his father's stern yet compassionate gaze flashed before his eyes. They were his pillars of strength, his unwavering support through the challenges of military service. Yet Aurangzeb knew that sharing the burden of his inner turmoil would only cause them undue worry and pain. Ammi, with her gentle demeanour, would fret endlessly, while his father, a seasoned veteran, would recognize the signs of unrest despite Aurangzeb's best efforts to conceal them. As he boarded the bus at the Shopian bus stand, the familiar sights of bustling market stalls and buzzing pedestrians seemed strangely distant. As the wheels of the bus rolled, Aurangzeb sought refuge in the rhythmic hum of the engine and the passing blur of familiar landscapes. Hours passed in silence, but as each mile brought him closer to home, he felt mountains away from the inner peace that he desperately sought.

Hours later, the bus rolled into Poonch, greeted by well-known scenes and sounds of his hometown. Aurangzeb was overcome with anticipation and dread. His younger brother, Tariq, stood waiting at the bus terminus with a beaming smile.

Aurangzeb straightened his posture, preparing himself for the reunion as he got off the bus. 'Tariq,' he greeted warmly, though his smile didn't quite reach his eyes. They embraced briefly, a gesture of camaraderie that momentarily eased the tension in Aurangzeb's chest. Together, they navigated the bustling streets of Poonch towards Salani, the sights and sounds of their hometown was like a bittersweet reminder of simpler times. Market vendors greeted them with affection while children played in the dusty alleyways and elderly men gathered at street corners to share stories of days gone by. For a transient moment, Aurangzeb allowed himself to be swept up in the familiar rhythms of home. Just then, Tariq stopped the bike at the Poonch market to buy supplies for home. Aurangzeb then decided to drive until Salani. As the two of them embarked on the bike journey from Poonch to Salani, the town enveloped him like a comforting embrace. They rode past narrow lanes lined with weathered stone houses— their roofs adorned with terracotta tiles that glistened in the afternoon sun. The air, crisp and refreshing, carried the fragrance of pine and wildflowers that flourished along the roadside. Aurangzeb's hands gripped the handles of the bike firmly, the rhythmic hum of the engine harmonizing with the symphony of nature around him. As they navigated through the gentle curves and rolling hills, memories of his childhood flooded back—carefree days spent playing cricket with his brothers and friends, in the dusty fields nearby and exploring hidden trails that wound through dense forests reverberating with the calls of birds and rustling leaves.

On every cherished leave from his military duties, Aurangzeb's first pilgrimage in Salani was to the masjid, where he found solace in the midst of his fast-paced military responsibilities and family life. The masjid stood at the heart of the village, its green and white painted walls and minarets reaching skyward, as a symbol of spiritual strength and community unity.

On reaching Krishna Ghati, Aurangzeb ventured on a narrow, unkempt road that snaked its way through verdant hillsides dotted with wildflowers and ancient trees. As he approached Salani, the village emerged like a hidden gem nestled in the embrace of the mountains. Houses, clustered on terraced steps carved from rugged terrain, cascaded down the slopes in a harmonious blend of tradition and natural beauty. Each home bore the weathered marks of time while narrow alleyways and stone staircases connected the labyrinthine pathways that wound through the village.

Approaching the masjid, Aurangzeb's footsteps echoed softly on the worn stone steps leading to its entrance. The courtyard was a sanctuary of tranquillity, shaded by ancient trees that offered respite from the midday sun. The call to prayer echoed melodiously through the village, drawing worshippers from all corners to gather in devotion and duty. Inside the masjid, the atmosphere was one of reverence and humility. Sunlight filtered through stained glass windows, casting colourful patterns on the intricately woven prayer rugs that lined the prayer hall. Aurangzeb found a quiet corner to perform ablutions, cleansing himself physically and spiritually before stepping into the sanctum of prayer.

As he stood shoulder to shoulder with fellow worshippers, Aurangzeb felt a profound sense of connection—a bond that transcended individual concerns and united the community in shared faith. The imam's voice resonated with serenity as he recited verses from the Quran, each word a reminder of divine guidance and grace.

In the moments of prayer, Aurangzeb poured out his heart, seeking strength and guidance in the face of his duties as a soldier. He prayed for forgiveness and offered heartfelt supplications for courage, protection and wisdom. His thoughts drifted to the emotional challenges and familial responsibilities that awaited him beyond the sanctuary walls.

After completing his prayers, Aurangzeb remained in the masjid a while longer, finding solace in the peace that enveloped him. He listened to the murmurs of conversations that reverberated through the courtyard, exchanged warm greetings with familiar faces and shared moments of quiet contemplation with himself.

Leaving the masjid, Aurangzeb and Tariq made their way to their ancestral home, walking through the winding roads adorned with similar-looking houses on one side and a vast expanse of valley and ridge on the other. From Salani's vantage point, Aurangzeb gazed across the majestic mountains that stretched into the distance, their peaks kissing the sky, and felt a deep connection to the land and its timeless beauty. He realized that the mountains overlooking the border with Pakistan had been silent witnesses to countless skirmishes, where lives were lost and echoes of conflict reverberated.

With their silent vigil over Salani, the mountains became a symbol of resilience and strength, a testament to the enduring ties that bound Aurangzeb to his homeland and the values that guided his journey as a soldier and son of Salani. Just as they had weathered the tumultuous history of the region without faltering, Aurangzeb too knew he must confront his own battles with courage and determination. He decided, each day from then on, as he would don his olive-green uniform prepared to face new challenges, he would find strength in the silent wisdom of the mountain—a reminder that, despite the hardships and sacrifices, his duty as a soldier demanded unwavering commitment. Aurangzeb knew that he had committed far too many mistakes in the past, and it was now time for redemption.

As he made his way home, the setting sun painted the horizon in shades of crimson and gold, casting a warm glow over the village. At last, they arrived at his family home—a modest yet sturdy structure with walls coated in thick mud, giving it an earthy, rustic charm. The mud smoothed over time with caring hands had formed irregular patterns that reflected the sun's warmth in shades of ochre and brown. The roof was thatched gently sloping downward, made from dried straw intricately woven.

As was customary, Raj Begum and Hanief stood outside the door, their faces radiant with joy and relief at the sight of their son returning home. Raj Begum's eyes glistened with unshed tears as she embraced Aurangzeb tightly, her soft words of welcome carrying a mother's unconditional love. Hanief clasped Aurangzeb's shoulder with a firm grip, his silent pride evident in the warmth of his gaze. They exchanged a brief nod—a quiet acknowledgement of the unspoken bond between father and son, forged through shared sacrifices and a deep-rooted commitment to duty.

Inside the welcoming warmth of their home, the scent of ammi's cooking filled the air—the aroma of fresh white butter and warm milk was indeed a feast to celebrate Aurangzeb's homecoming.

Seated around the rustic stove, they shared tea, with conversations flowing effortlessly, ranging from mundane everyday happenings to profound musings of life. His parents sat across from him, their expressions a blend of relief and concern. Ammi poured tea with practised grace. Aurangzeb observed their every movement, grateful for their silent understanding, yet fearful of the turmoil erupting beneath his calm façade. He sipped his tea, the warmth of the golden liquid spreading through his chest like a transient comfort. The fragrant brew offered a brief reprieve from the weight of his memories, a momentary distraction from the faces of innocent lives lost that haunted his thoughts.

Yet, despite his efforts to mask his predicament, Aurangzeb couldn't shake the fear that his parents might see through this made-up hard exterior. Their eyes, lined with years of experience and love, could scan his soul for answers. Occasionally, a lull would descend upon the conversation, filled only by the soft clinking of teaspoons against porcelain and the distant sounds of evening settling over the household. In those moments, Aurangzeb felt the weight of his grief press against his chest, threatening to spill forth in a torrent of unspoken words and pent-up emotions.

As the tea grew cold in his cup, Aurangzeb realized that despite his fear and anguish, this simple act of sharing tea with his parents had helped him cross the bridge and embark on the journey of healing.

Soon, the sound of youthful footsteps grew prominent. Aurangzeb's younger siblings burst into the room, their faces flushed with excitement and curiosity. With school bags slung over their shoulders and tales of their day tumbling from their lips, they raced towards him, their embrace filled with unabashed joy and adoration. Their innocence and boundless energy were a stark contrast to Aurangzeb's own weariness. Yet, their presence was a balm to his soul, reminding him of the purity of familial love and the resilience of childhood bonds. He found himself swept up in their chatter, their stories weaving a tapestry of shared memories and dreams.

The siblings showed Aurangzeb their school projects and recounted tales of playground triumphs. As the evening unfolded, he found himself caught between past and present, grief and gratitude. His parents' gentle reassurances and siblings' unquestioning love created a safe haven where he could begin to reconcile his conflicted emotions. The weight on his chest lightened, if only for a moment, as he allowed himself to be fully present. The turmoil that had plagued him seemed distant, overshadowed by the simple yet profound joy of being reunited with those who mattered most.

That evening, dinner was laid in the comforting embrace of Aurangzeb's childhood home. Ammi's makke ki roti, cooked to golden perfection and adorned with a generous dollop of fresh butter and a sprinkling of jaggery powder, held a special place in Aurangzeb's heart. For him, this simple meal transcended the need for extravagant spreads—it was a feast of nostalgia and love, served on humble plates but rich in familial bonds.

As they ate, conversation flowed naturally, punctuated by moments of shared laughter. Raj Begum's eyes sparkled with pride as she observed Aurangzeb enjoying her culinary creation, while Hanief's occasional nods of approval conveyed a silent understanding that surpassed words. Amid this intimate gathering, Aurangzeb found himself immersed in a blend of emotions—gratitude for his family's unwavering support, nostalgia for simpler times and a deep-seated longing for peace in the thick of the turmoil of his recent experiences. Each bite of the comforting meal seemed to nourish not just his body but also his soul, bridging the gap between past and present with every morsel. Outside, the night settled over the world in a blanket of tranquillity, casting a soft glow through the windows that framed their shared moments of togetherness. As the dinner concluded in the warm embrace of familial love, the night unfurled its velvet tapestry outside. A gentle breeze carried the scent of night-blooming flowers, mingling with the crisp, earthy fragrance of dew-kissed grass. Above, the moon hung like a silver lantern in the ink-black sky, casting its soft, ethereal glow over the world below.

Aurangzeb stepped outside into the cool embrace of the night; his head filled with the nostalgic pull of familiar traditions. Outside, he found his young siblings preparing their woven wooden beds, arranged in a neat row under the watchful gaze of the moon. The wooden frames of the bed, weathered with time yet lovingly maintained, cradled the intricate woven patterns that told stories of craftsmanship and heritage. The beds were not just places to rest one's weary body but repositories of shared memories and unspoken bonds. From childhood tales spun in whispered conspiracies to solemn promises made under the stars, these beds had witnessed the ebb and flow of life within the family.

Despite the passage of time and the inevitability of change, this one tradition remained constant—sleeping under the starlit sky till the months of acute cold. Aurangzeb traced his fingers along the smooth frame of his cot, feeling the faint indentations left by years of use. The scent of polished wood mingled with the earthy fragrance of the garden around, creating an olfactory tapestry that transported him back to the countless nights spent beneath this celestial canopy.

As Aurangzeb lay cocooned beneath the patchwork blanket on his woven bed, the soft murmur of his siblings' voices drifted through the night air, mingling with the rustle of leaves and the distant song of crickets. As it is, Aurangzeb had been dreading the nights for the last couple of days, but he was rather jittery that particular night. Despite the serene backdrop, his mind was restless, consumed by thoughts of Ilham. Aurangzeb fidgeted with his phone, the screen casting a soft glow on his face as he unlocked it, his fingers hovering over the keys. Thoughts of Ilham tugged at his heart—her laughter, the sparkle in her eyes, the way she would effortlessly light up a room by her mere presence. He couldn't deny the fact that he loved her, but his mind was consumed with uncertainty. He had definitely sinned by ignoring the love of his life, but did he want her to see him in a state of turmoil? He didn't even know whether she still shared his feelings. Also, would she understand the turbulence he carried within him, forged by the rigours of military duty and the weight of unspoken emotions?

After what felt like an eternity, he typed out a message: 'As-salaam alaikum! Sab khairiyat? Chutti pe ghar aaya hoon' (Hello! Hope all is well with you. I have come home on leave). It felt like he was typing a message to some stranger, which ached him. While his thumb hovered over the send button, his heart raced with the mix of hope and fear. With a hesitant press, he sent the message, watching intently as the grey ticks turned to powder blue. It was a leap of faith. The moon, a silent witness to his inner upheaval, cast its silvery light over him like a benevolent guardian. Aurangzeb turned his phone face down as if shielding himself from the vulnerability laid bare in his message. Thoughts raced through his mind like shooting stars in the night sky—*What if she didn't reply? Was he too late? Was she even here anymore?* Aurangzeb wondered. And the most haunting thought of all—*what if she had moved on, leaving him adrift in a sea of unrequited longing, as he had not responded to any of her calls or letters, and of late, there was silence from her end as well.* Love was a feeling Aurangzeb was acquainted with. He, of course, loved Ilham, but did she still love him? Did she still want him in his life? Very well, now he had another thought to push him on the rollercoaster. Every notification sound on his phone made him jump with eagerness, only to deflate with disappointment when it turned out to be yet another distraction—a loan advertisement or a friend's casual message. He longed for Ilham's response, his heart skipping a beat at the mere possibility of her words lighting up his screen with warmth.

As he lay there, vulnerable yet hopeful, Aurangzeb realized that love, like courage, required risking his heart. Each passing moment felt like an eternity as he wrestled with his emotions. Love meant risking rejection, embracing the unknown and trusting in the possibility of reciprocation. For Aurangzeb, whose life had been shaped by duty and honour, this vulnerability felt both exhilarating yet daunting. But should he even talk about love? Had he known what love is, he wouldn't have been standing at the crossroads. As he tossed and turned on his bed, his thoughts were a jumble of emotions centred around Ilham, the girl who had

Rifleman Aurangzeb
at his company
location in Shopian

Rifleman Aurangzeb at his forward post in Kashmir

Aurangzeb with his fellow soldier during the convoy move

Aurangzeb really enjoyed stealing a few moments to get his pictures clicked

Aurangzeb with his soldiers patrolling the local town

The final salute at Salani

A large gathering at Aurangzeb's village, Salani, to bid him a tearful adieu

Aurangzeb's brothers carrying him on his final journey

Aurangzeb's mortal remains reached Salani on the day of Eid in 2018

People from all over the country reached Salani to pay their respects

Scene at Aurangzeb's native home before the helicopter landed

Mohammad Hanief and Raj Begum inconsolable after seeing the mortal remains of their son

Mohammad Hanief consoling his wife and giving her strength

Raj Begum embracing Aurangzeb's coffin

Mazar in Salani where the family would pray before every military operation of Aurangzeb's

Tariq praying at the mazar

Former defence
minister Nirmala
Sitaraman with the
family of Rifleman
Aurangzeb after
his demise

Raj Begum would
spend hours
looking at the
path Aurangzeb
would take on
his way home

L to R (Rubeena, Shazia,
Shahnaaz, Zafar, Asim,
Ayaan and Qasim)

Author visited Aurangzeb's
grave in Salani

Author with Aurangzeb's parents and siblings Tariq and Shabbir

Tariq and Shabbir joined the Indian Army after the demise of their brother Aurangzeb

Tariq and Shabbir with their mother on the day of their Kasam Parade

Years later, Asim also joined the Indian Army

Zafar and Raj Begum
with Asim on his Kasam
Parade in Srinagar

L to R
(Zafar and Asim)

10 May 2023: Mohammad
Hanief and Raj Begum
received the prestigious
Shaurya Chakra (P)
on behalf of Rifleman
Aurangzeb by the
Honourable President of
India Droupadi Murmu

*Photos courtesy of Rifleman Aurangzeb's family*

unknowingly captured his heart and eventually became his everything.

Meanwhile, a few streets away, Ilham sat in her room, her phone screen illuminating her thoughtful expression. She hadn't heard from Aurangzeb for a few months, and even though all their previous message interactions had been sporadic, each exchange left an indelible mark on her heart. She had tried incredibly hard to get over him and move on. But every time her mind would run away, her heart would race back to Aurangzeb. It was a spiral that she couldn't escape from. Then, the most unexpected thing happened. Her pulse raced as she read Aurangzeb's latest text—a simple announcement of his leave sparked a cascade of questions and hopes. She had, of course, deleted his number, but she remembered every digit like the back of her hand.

Did he think of her while he was away? Did he feel the same pull towards her that she felt towards him? The mixed signals he occasionally sent only added to her confusion. Was everything that he did before getting commissioned merely an act? Or was this message an attempt to act again? Was this message a simple update or a subtle invitation to something more? Did he want to see her, to explore what might blossom between them?

Despite her typically confident demeanour, Ilham hesitated. The vulnerability of opening her heart to him again was daunting. Ilham felt like a lone bird perched on a swaying branch, unsure whether to take flight into the vast known or remain grounded in the safety of familiarity. Yet, she knew with unwavering certainty that she didn't want to leave anything to what-ifs, and if she had even the slightest possibility of a future with Aurangzeb, she was ready to take the plunge and reply. Her fingers hovered over the keys, her heart racing with longing. She wanted answers and she deserved closure, if not love.

Finally, with a hesitant smile, Ilham typed her reply: '*Wa-Alaikum-Salaam. Kal shaam paanch baje Nadi ke pass milte hain. Goodnight*' (Hello! Let's meet at the riverside around 5 in the evening tomorrow. Goodnight). She hit send, her heart pounding in her chest as she second-guessed her decision. Was she too forward? Would Aurangzeb misinterpret her eagerness as something she didn't intend? The weight of her uncertainty hung in the air, mingling with the sweet scent of wildflowers drifting through her window. Yet, amidst the swirl of doubts, Ilham found a quiet determination. She knew that the answers wouldn't come from overthinking but from the unspoken language of their meeting—the way Aurangzeb's eyes would meet hers, the tenderness of his voice, the sincerity woven into the curve of his smile. As she prepared for bed, anticipation tingled in every nerve. Would Aurangzeb come? Would their meeting be the beginning of something new or a gentle closure to what could have been?

Aurangzeb's heart skipped a beat as he read Ilham's reply. Her words, simple yet filled with a quiet resolve, stirred a mixture of emotions within him—hope, anticipation and a tinge of apprehension. He couldn't deny the flutter of excitement that rose in his chest, knowing that he'd be meeting Ilham the following day. Setting his phone aside, Aurangzeb tried to calm the racing thoughts that threatened to overwhelm him. As fatigue finally claimed him, Aurangzeb drifted into a fitful sleep. Yet, instead of dreams of tranquil moments by the riverbank with Ilham, his slumber was invaded by restless nightmares of past operations. The faces of innocent lives lost, the reverberating gunfire and the weight of responsibility bore down on him like a relentless storm. In his sleep, he fought battles anew, each memory a haunting reminder of sacrifices made and lives forever altered. Even in sleep, his mind waged a war of its own—a struggle between duty and desire, between the scars of yesterday and the fragile hope of tomorrow. Amidst the turmoil of his nightmares, one image remained clear—the reading of Ilham's message, a flicker of hope that beckoned him towards a future where the burdens of the past could be at least, eased by the warmth of understanding and companionship.

In another world, Ilham pictured their meeting—the soft light of the setting sun casting a golden halo around them, the tranquil riverbank where they had agreed to meet adorned in the warm hues of the evening sun. She imagined the moment their eyes would finally meet, exchanging unspoken truths that words alone couldn't convey. Would she see the flicker of longing mirrored in Aurangzeb's eyes, a reflection of the emotions she had dared to nurture in her own heart? She was, of course, upset, but she had seen a side of Aurangzeb that only she knew. For her, he was this man with a tender heart and a firm resolve. She wasn't okay with him ghosting her, but all she wanted to know was whether he still loved her.

Despite the uncertainties that danced on the edges of her thoughts, Ilham felt a calm certainty blooming within—a belief that this meeting held the promise of clarity, of understanding, and perhaps of a future where their hearts might beat in rhythm together. Ilham held onto this newfound resolve as she closed her eyes, surrendering to the lull of sleep. Tomorrow awaited with its mysteries and possibilities, and she couldn't wait for the sun to rise the following morning.

# 7

# Pakistan: Rally of Masood Azhar

The morning unfolded with a quiet solemnity as Aurangzeb prepared for the day ahead. The usual sounds of his household—the clinking of utensils, the aroma of brewing tea—seemed distant, muffled by the overwhelming thoughts that consumed him. His mother's hand moved with practised grace, kneading the dough for chapatis, while his father hummed a tune as he brewed tea. The aroma of spices and freshly baked bread filled the air, enveloping the kitchen in a warm embrace. Aurangzeb tried to immerse himself in these mundane tasks, yet his mind incessantly wandered to the evening ahead. Time seemed to stretch endlessly, each minute passing like a slow-moving river, carrying with it the weight of his apprehensions and hopes. He checked his watch repeatedly, unable to quell the restless stirrings within him. As the morning shifted to noon, Aurangzeb found himself unable to wait any longer. The walls of his home felt confining, suffocating even, as the anticipation loomed large. Aurangzeb immediately rushed to his room and removed a crisp black mandarin collar shirt from his rucksack. Black shirt-blue jeans would be the safest combination now that he couldn't think straight. As he stepped out, the fragrance of musk followed him. Zafar, sitting on the patio, observed Aurangzeb's every move. Ironed clothes, hair neatly in place, drenched in the scent of musk and a faint smile on his face— there was enough evidence for Zafar to believe that something was not quite right.

'*Aurangzeb bhai, kahan jaa rahe ho? Main bhi chalta hoon*' (Aurangzeb brother, where are you going? I shall also accompany you), Zafar exclaimed, rising from his comfort spot. He waited for Aurangzeb's attempt at deception. '*Umm…Main bus yahin dost ke pass jaa raha hun, tum kya karoge?*' (Umm…I am just going to meet my friend. What will you do there?), Aurangzeb avoided eye contact as if in a rush.

The route to the river bank felt longer than ever, or maybe his steps were slower. He had longed to see Ilham, but he didn't know what to say to her. He was guilty; nobody deserved to be treated like that, especially not Ilham. She was the reason Aurangzeb learnt the difference between living and surviving. She gently coaxed out the child in him. His eyes were desperate to meet hers. And there, breaking the golden light of the sun, walked Ilham, looking ethereal in a white suit with intricate powder blue weave. Aurangzeb didn't know if he still had the right to hug her, but he stepped forward; Ilham glanced at him and moved aside, resting on the wooden bench on the side. All was not well; he knew, and what was he expecting? While the two sat in silence, the sounds of the river rustling with the rocks played in the backdrop. Aurangzeb turned towards her and held her hand. '*Tum yahan dekhoge bhi nahi?* (Will you not even look at me?) Ilham looked as her eyes welled up. '*Main galat hoon. Mujhse balance nahi hui life. Par main yeh nahi bolunga ki tum mujhse behtar deserve karti ho. Tum sirf mujhe deserve karti ho and main tumhare layak ban kar dikhaunga. Sirf, ek chance, please*' (I am wrong. I couldn't balance my military life and my personal life. I will not say that you deserve someone better. You deserve me, and I will prove worthy of you. Just give me one chance, please). Aurangzeb wiped her tears as his own eyes shed a few. There was no denying the fact that Aurangzeb wasn't there when Ilham fought her fear or when she cried herself to sleep. She kept calling incessantly without a hello in reply. There was no denying the fact that she was hurt, and while usually, she wouldn't see the person again who made her feel unworthy, it was Aurangzeb, the man she loved. She tried to hate him for days, but her heart kept loving him more. Aurangzeb gave Ilham some of the most heart-wrenching days of her life, but he also gave her reasons to believe in fairytales; he made her believe that there exists one perfect match for everyone, like the missing piece of a puzzle. For Ilham, he was the missing piece. After she lashed out at him, he apologized profusely, as if tomorrow depended on it, and soon they found themselves back in each other's embrace. Such is the power of love. You may think you have lost everything on this journey of life, but just when you are about to give up, love knocks. For some, the journey may be fraught with a few wrong turns, but ultimately, your destination will pull you close like a magnet to a metal. Aurangzeb finally found his purpose; he would continue his military duties but with Ilham by his side. He confided in her about his fears and nightmares, and she, being the woman that she was, took away all his sorrow and gave him all the happiness in the world. Aurangzeb promised Ilham that she would be central to his life, and it was time for them to take the next step. Ilham was elated beyond belief to learn that Aurangzeb had decided to inform the families about their fondness for each other in the coming Eid. She couldn't believe his words. Their story had not ended, it was just a turn of the page. Aurangzeb and Ilham were meant to be or were they?

While in one part of the world, Aurangzeb and Ilham were experiencing a beautiful phase in their lives—dreaming of a life together, to celebrate, to cherish, to hold one another—in another part, across the line of control, schemes were meticulously devised to bring about Aurangzeb's tragic fate.

In the aftermath of the operation where Tallah Rashid was executed, significant recoveries by the Indian Army unveiled a trail leading back to Pakistan. Among the cache of supplies seized, were numerous items marked 'Made in Pakistan', underscoring a direct cross-border link to the missions. These findings hinted at a direct link stretching across the line of control, implicating support and involvement from across the border. Among the recovered items was a US-made M4 Carbine Rifle, an elite weapon typically reserved for Pakistan's military force. Its presence in the hands of the militants unveiled a troubling nexus between state-backed actors and insurgent groups, further escalating international scrutiny and diplomatic tensions. In the aftermath of the mission, the Indian authorities swiftly convened a press conference to disclose the findings and implications of the operation. Against the backdrop of a meticulously laid out display of seized weapons and caches, senior military officials addressed a packed room of journalists and international observers. The spokesperson for the Indian Army, flanked by maps on either side detailing the operations coordinates and photographs of recovered supplies, began with a stern acknowledgement of the objectives of the operation and the challenges faced by Indian security forces in combating cross-border militancy. With measured words, the spokesperson pressed upon the significance of the recovered weaponry, emphasizing its direct linkage to Pakistan and its state military apparatus. The press conference escalated into a formal demand directed towards Pakistan. 'We call upon the Pakistan government to accept responsibility for its role in supporting and arming militant outfits such as Jaish-e-Mohammed,' the spokesperson continued, calling for Pakistan to claim the bodies of those militants who had fallen in the operation.[38] The call was not merely procedural but also a strategic move aimed at compelling accountability on the international stage. It signalled India's resolve to expose and challenge Pakistan's alleged indulgence in cross-border terrorism, further bolstered by concrete evidence obtained during the Tallah Rashid operation. As the press conference concluded, the images of seized weaponry and the impassioned statements were repeatedly flashed through global media channels, igniting debates and diplomatic responses from the capitals around the world. The call for accountability resonated beyond the confines of South Asia, reflecting the enduring impact of cross-border militancy on regional stability and international relations.

---

[38] 'Will Ask Pak To Collect Body of Azhar's Nephew: IGP', Kashmir Observer, 7 November 2017, https://kashmirobserver.net/2017/11/07/will-ask-pak-tocollect-body-of-azhar%C2%92s-nephew-igp/.

## Bahawalpur, Pakistan

The news of Tallah Rashid's demise spread swiftly across the LoC, reaching the shadowy corridors of power in Bahawalpur, Pakistan. Here, nestled within a labyrinth of dusty streets, guarded by high walls adorned with surveillance cameras, lay the fortress-like mansion of Masood Azhar—a bastion of both opulence and secrecy. The mansion was fortified with high walls topped with razor wire, punctuated by guarded gates and surveillance cameras that monitored every approach. A team of heavily armed security personnel maintained a vigilant watch, their presence concealed within the lush greenery and manicured gardens that surrounded the estate.

Masood Azhar's mansion was a blend of traditional and modern architecture, with intricate carvings decorating its grand façade and towering minarets. The entrance was massive with ornate pillars and a grand doorway, hinting at the wealth and influence that Masood Azhar commanded in his circle. Inside, the mansion unfolded into a series of lavish chambers and halls with Persian carpets laid out meticulously, and exquisite tapestries and priceless artworks placed in every corner. Chandeliers hung from high ceilings, casting a soft amber glow over the rooms furnished with elegant sofas and antique carved furniture. The scent of incense lingered in the air, mingling with the aroma of freshly brewed tea served by attendants in traditional attire. It was appalling how a man with the blood of countless innocent people on his hands was living a life of such luxury within the periphery of Pakistan. A man who was a most wanted militant in India; a man for whom China vetoed against the demand of the United Nations to have him declared an international criminal, commanded such loyalty from the Pakistani government.

They are alive, believe them to be alive, consider them alive. Yes, your limited intellect cannot comprehend this life of theirs, but just as you believe in the Throne without having seen it, it is necessary to believe that both the Throne and the Chair exist... And similarly, it is essential to believe that the Martyr is alive.
Salutations to the passionate one!
For a martyr, Allah has 5 special rewards:

1. **Before the first drop of blood, his place in Paradise is shown to him**
2. **He is saved from the terror of the grave**
3. **On the Day of Judgment, he remains safe from great fear**
4. **A crown of honour is placed on his head, which is better than all the worldly treasures**
5. **He will marry 72 beautiful companions (hoors)**

Bring that disobedient person here who has led my nephew and our friends to Paradise.

*Having sacrificed everything in the path of love,*
*The people of the heart are so happy,*
*As if they have gained the wealth of the entire universe.*
*The king of the garden took pride in his own springs,*
*But when they arrived, they spread over all the springs.*

The audio file, carefully scripted and recorded in a secure location, served as a rallying cry to indoctrinate and mobilize the youth, who were seen as vital recruits in his fight for the so-called liberation of Kashmir. In it, Masood Azhar vividly

On the fateful day when the news of Tallah Rashid's demise hushed through the mansion, Masood Azhar was ensconced in his private study—a bastion within the mansion where he conducted all his strategic affairs and received updates from his network of operatives spread across the valley.

He sat at an enormous mahogany desk, its surface scattered with maps, correspondence from sympathizers and a metal brass lamp that cast a warm yellow glow across his weathered face. Panelled with dark wood, the walls were lined with shelves that sagged under the weight of leather-bound volumes nestled alongside stacks of handwritten notes. On one wall behind his expansive desk, hung a large map of the Kashmir valley, meticulously marked with coloured pins and annotations. Each pin denoted a significant location—a strategic stronghold in the valley, a sympathetic village, military installations, routes of ingress and egress or a potential target. The map was evidence of Masood Azhar's attention to detail and his strategic mind, which constantly plotted and reevaluated the chessboard of destruction. It was not just a geographical representation but a canvas upon which Masood Azhar stretched his dreams of destabilizing India's hold over the region of Kashmir. Alongside the maps, sketches and diagrams adorned the wall, depicting various scenarios of insurgency and resistance. These were not just theoretical musings but practical blueprints born from years of covert operations and intelligence gathering. Detailed plans for infiltrating border crossings, disrupting communication networks, and inciting local unrest were meticulously laid out in intricate details, which showed Masood Azhar's grasp over asymmetrical warfare. What Masood Azhar failed to notice was that India as a country is not so fragile that it can be broken by some self-proclaimed godman sitting across the fence, but of course, a man could dream. As he received the news of Tallah Rashid's demise, the room seemed to contract around him, enclosing him in a bubble of solemnity. His brows furrowed momentarily, showing a rare glimpse of vulnerability beneath the mask of stoicism that he often wore. He slowly rose from his chair, his hands gripping the edge of the desk as if to steady himself against the weight of the news. The silence in the room was palpable, broken only by the distant sounds of the mansion's guards patrolling the grounds outside. In that sombre moment, Masood Azhar made a decision. His voice, typically grim and measured, now resonated with a steely determination as he recorded an audio message for his followers and supporters.[39] His words carried both mourning for the fallen and a call to rise against those they perceived as their enemies.

*Mere bhanje Tallah Rashid ki maut bekar nahi jayegi. Jannat mein usse ucch sthan milega. Shaheed ke marne ka inkaar nahi, voh zaroor mara hai, lekin unke murda hone ka inkar hai. Voh maut aane ke baad bhi murda nahi hua. Inhe murda kahoge toh Quran ke nafarmaan, inhe murda samjhoge toh Quran ke nafarmaan. Toh phir hum inhe kya samjhein? Voh zinda hai, inhe zinda maano, inhe zinda samjho. Haan unki yeh zindagi tumhari mehdood akal se samjhi nahi jaa sakti, magar tumne na arsh dekha hain na kursi par yakeen rakhna zaroori hai ki arsh bhi hai aur kursi*

---

[39] 'Masood Azhar releases an audio clip after his nephew Talha Rasheed killed in an encounter', IndiaTV, 10 November 2017, https://www.youtube.com/watch?v=Nhyb8uEsYqw.

*bhi . . . Aur issi tarah yeh yakeen rakhna lazmi hai ki shaheed zinda hai.*

*Deewane ko salaam!*
*Shaheed ke liye allah taala ke pass 5 inam hain: -*

1) *Khoon ke pehle katre ke saath jannat mein uska makaam dikha diya jata hai*
2) *Usse Azaad -e- Kabr se bacha liya jata hai*
3) *Qayamat ke din ke badi ghabrahat se voh mehfooz rehta hai*
4) *Uske sarr par Waqar ka Taaj rakha jata hai, jo duniya ki tamaan cheezon se behtar hai*
5) *72 hoorein jinse uska nikaah kar diya jayega*

*Tum uss nafarmaan shaks ko le aao, jinhone mere bhanjhe, humare doston ko jannat pahunchaya hai.*

**Sab kuch luta ke. Rah-e-mohabbat mein ahale dil,**
**Khush hain ki jaise Daulat-e-Konain paa gaye,**
**Shahne chaman ko apni baharon pe naaz tha,**
**voh aa gaye,**
**Toh saari baharon pe chaa gaye**

The death of my nephew Tallah Rashid will not go in vain. He will attain a high place in Paradise. There is no denial of a martyr's death; indeed, he has surely died. But to deny them the status of a martyr after his death is to disobey the Quran. If you call them dead, it is disobedience to the Quran. If you consider them dead, it is disobedience to the Quran. So then, how should we understand them?

portrayed a world where resistance and martyrdom held more promise than complacency and submission. He appealed to the youth's sense of unity and belonging, invoking historical grievances and religious duty to spur them into action.

His rhetoric, although steeped in emotional appeal, also contained a subtle desperation—a recognition of the mounting challenges faced by the militants in Kashmir, particularly since the Indian Army's intensified Operation All Out.[40] Knowing the importance and timing of the narrative surrounding Tallah Rashid's death, Masood Azhar instructed his spokesperson, Hassan Shah, to issue an official statement to the local news agencies. Hassan Shah's statement confirmed Tallah Rashid's identity as a slain militant and emphasized his role as a martyr in the cause of liberation—a narrative designed to inspire sympathy and solidarity amongst the populace. Furthermore, Masood Azhar saw the moment as an opportunity to consolidate his support base and demonstrate his enduring influence in Bahawalpur. He directed Hassan Shah to organize a rally in the city within the next two days—a gathering intended not only to honour Tallah Rashid's memory but also to reaffirm Jaish-e-Mohammed's presence and relevance.

The rally in Bahawalpur, meticulously planned and promoted through local channels, drew a large turnout of supporters from across the region. The venue, a cricket ground

---

[40] Operation All Out (OAO) is a joint offensive launched by Indian security forces to flush out militants and terrorists from Kashmir until there is complete peace in the state. The operation typically involves coordinated efforts with other security forces and intelligence agencies to target and apprehend or eliminate insurgents, thereby restoring peace and security in the affected areas.

on the city's outskirts, buzzed with anticipation as people arrived in droves, driven by loyalty and shared belief. Masood Azhar, dressed in his characteristic white robe and head covered with a black and white checkered scarf, took to the makeshift stage amidst chants and cheers. As he approached the centre, a hush fell over the crowd, with anticipation hanging in the air. The crowd eagerly awaited to hear the man who had just lost his nephew to the Indian forces. Microphones awaited his voice, amplifying the weight of his words to every corner of the vast gathering. He spoke about the martyrdom of their comrades, about how they must collectively rise against what they believed to be atrocities against their brothers and sisters in Kashmir. His words struck a chord among the assembled throngs, eliciting murmurs of agreement and cries of anger. Banners waved more vigorously, their messages of resistance fluttering defiantly against the backdrop of the clear sky. Azhar's voice rang with conviction as he said that for every life taken, for every drop of blood of their own spilt, they would take revenge. Furthermore, his proclamation of a reward for avenging his nephew's and other comrades' deaths with a promise of 20 lakh stirred emotions, further igniting a fresh determination among the spectators. As he continued speaking, the crowd erupted into chaos and chants. Some raised clenched fists and others waved flags that displayed the emblem of their cause. At that moment, Masood Azhar stood not just as a leader but as a messiah, a crusader in their war for Kashmiri liberation.

Oblivious to the widespread propaganda across the line of control, Aurangzeb returned to his unit location with a healed heart, a future full of promises, and of course, love.

After getting back with Ilham, Aurangzeb's life took on a whole new meaning. He began to question the priorities he had always held so tightly. While military missions had always given him a rush of excitement, he now found joy in quiet moments, thinking about life from Ilham's perspective. Though he still was the over-enthusiastic soldier, ready to take on any mission, his fondness for Ilham kept him grounded. Every soldier when he joins the forces, takes the oath to fight for the honour of the Indian tricolour till the peril of their life, but when a soldier falls in love, deep down subconsciously, he starts cultivating the fear of moving away from the love of his life. In that moment, Aurangzeb was going through the same transition. Ilham had shown him how to appreciate simplicity and the power of kindness, but it wasn't always easy. He struggled to balance his army duty and his growing feelings for Ilham. His responsibility to his fellow soldiers and his pledge to protect his country weighed heavily on his mind. Yet, loving Ilham taught him a new kind of bravery—the courage to be vulnerable and pursue his own dreams beyond the battlefield.

Of course, their relationship wasn't smooth sailing; they had their moments of doubt, distance and disagreements. Aurangzeb's first love, his uniform, and the nation would sometimes come in the way of his love for Ilham. Whenever he would be out for any military operation or to a forward post, Ilham's fingers wouldn't stop rolling on the prayer beads. Every night that Aurangzeb was fighting militants, Ilham fought her inner fears. She would wait for his 'all okay' call before hitting the bed. Life for a soldier is definitely not an easy walk, but for a woman who loves a soldier, it's an uphill battle. Only a woman who is fierce and fearless can love a man in the olive green. Ilham had to be the force, the Army who had to hold the fort back home while Aurangzeb fulfilled his duty towards the nation; an oath he took before donning the Indian Army uniform. Navigating the trials, Ilham and Aurangzeb found romance in his short leaves where every minute was precious and filled with the warmth of their love. No matter how brief, each phone call carried the weight of yearning and devotion. Handwritten letters, penned with love and longing, bridged the physical distance between them. As Aurangzeb looked into Ilham's eyes before every departure, he saw not just love but also courage and sacrifice. Her support was his anchor, grounding him in the belief that their love could weather any storm. He made it a point to call Ilham before every operation and surprise her on every leave.

# #8

# Books to Bullets:
# The Birth of Sameer Tiger

In the troubled valley of Kashmir, unrest had become an enduring challenge, exacerbated by recent events that had shaken the delicate peace. The death of Tallah Rashid had stirred a fresh wave of instability. Kashmir was once again in a cauldron of unrest. Political tensions simmered, protests filled the streets and the echoes of violence resounded through the valleys. The death of the notorious militant had not quelled the unrest; instead, it seemed to fan the flames of dissent and defiance across the region. Clashes between the security forces and militants became more frequent and intense, where each encounter left behind a trail of shattered peace and deepening wounds. Moreover, Masood Azhar's fiery public speech from Bahawalpur started showing results on the ground in Kashmir, as his words galvanized militant groups to intensify their attacks and incite incidents of stone pelting. Intelligence reports hinted at heightened military movements, prompting increased vigilance, especially in the Pulwama–Shopian belt of Kashmir, where 44 Rashtriya Rifles was patrolling regularly.

In the narrow lanes of Shopian, popularly called the apple bowl of Kashmir, where once the aroma of ripening apples mingled with the laughter of children, now lay a palpable sense of apprehension. The 44 Rashtriya Rifles, stalwart guardians of order, found themselves engulfed in a perpetual dance with the shadows in their area of responsibility. Each patrol of theirs passed through the narrow alleyways, a potential battleground fraught with the anticipation of ambush, as every corner invited possible confrontation with masked insurgents. The populace of Shopian, resilient yet weary by years of strife, navigated their lives amidst a landscape scarred by conflict. Curfews descended like a shroud over the bustling markets, silencing the rhythmic hum of commerce that once defined the town's heartbeat. What remained a matter of concern for the security forces were the clandestine meetings in remote hideouts and the ominous rustling of insurgent sympathizers among the civilian population. Amidst this volatile backdrop, Rifleman Aurangzeb found himself on one such patrol; his AK-47 slung over his shoulder as he and his company soldiers navigated the narrow lanes and bustling markets of Shopian. The early sun cast a golden glow over the scene—a group of young children, their backpacks slung over their shoulders, skipping along the dusty road towards their school. Their laughter and chatter filled the air, momentarily masking the tension that lingered beneath the surface. Aurangzeb watched them with a blend of nostalgia and concern.

'*Kabhi hum bhi aise he school jaate the. Bade masoom hote hain bache. Inhe mahaul ka kya pata*' (Look at them. Even we used to go to school like that. It seems like yesterday. There is innocence shining through their eyes as they are unaware of the dangers lurking around them), Aurangzeb told Rizwan, a fellow soldier as his voice tinged with remorse.

Rizwan nodded solemnly, his gaze following the children's carefree movements. *'Inki umar mein bachon ko khelna chahiye, bade bade sapne dekhne chahiye, naa ki faujiyon se ghiri sadkon ke beech se guzarna chahiye'* (Children their age should play games, dream about their future and not have to navigate through a conflict-ridden landscape), he replied softly.

*'Tallah Rashid jaise kayi atankiyon ne kitne bachon ka bachpan cheen liya hoga'* (The likes of Tallah Rashid would have robbed the innocence of quite a few children), Aurangzeb continued, his voice underscored with bitterness. *'Inka fayeda utha kar, apne naakam iradon mein inki bali chadha dete hain'* (They exploit their vulnerability, turning them into pawns in their deadly game).

Rizwan's jaw tightened with resolve. *'Humari duty hai inki raksha karna, Aurangzeb, taaki inhe ek achi zindagi jeene ka mauka mile, iss sabse door'* (It's our duty to protect them, Aurangzeb. To ensure that they have a chance at a better life, free from the influence of those who seek to destroy our homeland).

*'Tujhe pata hai kitne bache aaj ki date mein Hizbul Mujahideen, Jaish-e-Mohammed ya Lashkar mein recruited hain aur kayi toh commander bane baithe hain'* (Do you know that as on date, how many children are recruited by Hizbul Mujahideen, Jaish-e-Mohammed or Lashkar? Some have even risen in ranks to become commanders), Aurangzeb looked disappointed as they continued their patrol through the winding lanes of Shopian.

There, in the backdrop of the call to prayer from a distant mosque, Aurangzeb knew that the Tallah Rashid operation may have given a blow to the militants, but the battle to win over the hearts and minds of the valley's youth was far from over.

## 30 April 2018
## Drabgam, Pulwama

The sun had just begun to peek over the jagged peaks of the Pir Panjal range as three elderly men gathered at a roadside tea stall nestled along the village's main thoroughfare. Their breath misted in the cold air as they sipped on steaming cups of kahwa.[41] The front page of the anti-establishment local newspaper bore the headline that had become all too common in their region. Printed in black ink, 'Poster Boy of Kashmir Liberation Martyred', the headline screamed, drawing attention and stirring conversations that would delve into the depths of their community's recent turmoil. The news inevitably diverged their thoughts to Sameer—a name that had become synonymous with concern and controversy in their village.

Hafizullah, the eldest of the trio at the tea stall, was known for his wisdom and connection to the pulse of the community. He stirred his kahwa thoughtfully, his eyes narrowing as he began, '*Sameer hamesha se he alag mizaaj ka tha. Uske abu, Ahmed din raat uski chinta karte the, kaafi mushkil haalat paida karta tha voh*' (Sameer was always a trouble magnet. Ahmed, his father, worried for him day and night. Ever since he was a young boy, trouble seemed to follow him).

---

[41] A traditional drink in Kashmir made with tea leaves, crushed dry fruits, saffron and hot water.

Ali, the retired school teacher, nodded in agreement. '*Yaad hai jab Sameer ne apne chacha ke saari bhed bhaga di thi. Ek chante ke badle itna nuksaan kara tha*' (Remember, when Sameer had set all the cattle free at his uncle's place. It was after his uncle slapped him for some mischief). '*Sameer mein gussa hamesha se tha par voh apni hadd bhi nahi janta tha*' (The boy had a temper, you bet. There was more to it than that; he just didn't know his limits).

Rahim Khan, a former government clerk known for his meticulous attention to detail, leaned forward, his brows furrowed. '*Dekho, kya anjaam hua. Kuch log bata rahe the ki kuch saal pehle Ghulam Bhat se mila tha aur yeh uski seekh hain. Suna hai Ghulam Bhat police hirasat mein hai ab*' (And now, look where he's ended up. Some villagers were talking about how it was Ghulam Bhat's influence. I have heard that Ghulam Bhat is now in police custody as he would lure innocent children, promising them a game to heaven, as if martyrdom was some sort of salvation).

This conversation soon turned towards Sameer's father—a man who had invested his hopes in his son's education, hoping it would be their ticket out of the cycle of poverty and the unrest that shadowed their village. Unbeknownst to him, Sameer's journey soon took a darker turn, influenced by forces that would test familial bonds and reshape his role in the valley's tumultuous narrative.

Sameer was a young boy born and raised in the picturesque town of Drabgam, nestled in the heart of Pulwama district. His childhood was like that of many others in the area—filled with laughter, cricket matches in narrow alleys and the aroma of home-made Kashmiri cuisine wafting through the air. However, as he grew older, his path diverged from the traditional trajectory his parents had hoped for. Education was highly valued in Sameer's family, it being a luxury. His father, a janitor in the irrigation department, and his mother, a homemaker, dreamt of seeing him become a doctor or an engineer. Sameer showed promise in his early school years, often drawing praise for his sharp intellect and quick wit. But by the time he reached the eighth standard, something changed. The subjects that once intrigued him now seemed burdensome. His mind wandered during lessons and homework assignments piled up, untouched. The once bright-eyed student became disinterested and distant. Teachers and family members tried to encourage him, but Sameer couldn't find the motivation to excel academically, he just wasn't interested. He didn't see a point in education. It may be so because Sameer's childhood was shadowed by domestic strife. At Sameer's home, the air often crackled with the bitterness of arguments and the sound of harsh blows that eventually left deep scars on his young heart. The tumultuous environment at home left scars etched not only on the walls but also on young Sameer's impressionable mind. One such instance remained seared into Sameer's memory like a jagged shard of glass embedded in his consciousness.

It was a cool autumn evening when the flickering bulb cast long shadows across the worn carpets of their modest living room. Sameer, barely eight years old, cowered in a corner, as his small frame trembled watching his father's fists rain down upon his mother. The echoes of her cries thundered through the cramped space, mingling with the clatter of furniture overturned in a storm of rage. In those harrowing moments, Sameer's young heart swelled with a potent cocktail of fear and anger—a brew that would shape his perception of the world and his place within it. For him, the limits of anger were an enigma; he didn't know where to draw the line.

In Sameer's young mind, the concept of power took root early, shaped by the turbulent dynamics of his home and the stark realities of Kashmir's conflict-ridden streets. Growing up, he internalized a belief that men inherently possessed power, often manifested through dominance over women and the ability to assert their will unchecked. To Sameer, this became a blueprint for understanding power—the idea that men yielded power to do as they please and how women were submissive to men. This belief was reinforced by the presence of armed soldiers patrolling his village. To Sameer, the men in uniform seemed to command respect and instil fear (not their intention, of course) simply by virtue of their weapons. He observed how the villagers would scatter like startled birds at the sight of these uniformed men, their homes becoming sanctuaries of fear and caution. However absurd Sameer's ideas were, they were a result of his childhood traumas. In his young mind, a man with a gun was likened to a deity—someone to be feared, obeyed and revered. This perception of his extended to the militants as well who used to occasionally pass through the village. Despite their often-disruptive presence, some villagers treated them with respect, offering hospitality without question. This idea further cemented Sameer's belief that power and control stemmed from wielding force.

The psychological impact of these observations was profound. Sameer began to equate power with the ability to instil fear and command obedience through intimidation.

In his worldview, authority was not earned through merit or respect but asserted through the threat of violence. The sight of an AK-47 in someone's hand evoked a sense of reverence and superiority in Sameer's mind, a stark contrast to the peaceful tools of education and knowledge. In essence, Sameer's early experiences cultivated a belief that men, especially those armed, transcended more authority. The word 'power' became synonymous with control over others' lives and the ability to impose one's will without question. In his mind, the lesson was clear: bullets held more relevance than books in a world where conflict and uncertainty reigned. The AK-47 became an instrument of choice for those who sought to shape their environment through intimidation and dominance rather than through dialogue or discourse. He understood that to navigate the complexities of Kashmir's unrest, he would have to befriend the bullets and align himself with the forces of power and violence that were crucial for survival and dominance. Indeed, Sameer had descended a dark path shaped by his distorted perceptions and harsh realities, where any possibility of a U-turn seemed forbidden. When a child himself has moved towards the wrong path, it is easier for the sympathizers to pull him into their fold, manipulate them, and exploit their innocence and vulnerability.

In the quiet outskirts of Drabgam, nestled in the midst of ancient walnut trees, lived an old man known as Ghulam Bhat. To the casual observer, Ghulam appeared to be a weathered soul with a penchant for solitude, but beneath his grizzled exterior lay a cunning past—an ex-overground worker-turned-recruiter who now spent his days weaving tales of resistance and liberation to brainwash young minds.

Sameer, at the age of sixteen, had stumbled upon Ghulam's dwelling one misty morning while taking a shortcut to school. At first, their encounters were fleeting—a nod of acknowledgment or brief exchange of pleasantries. However, Sameer's curiosity expanded with each meeting, probably as he grappled with inner turmoil. Inside the dimly lit hut, the air hung heavy with the scent of wood smoke and the hushed anticipation of clandestine knowledge. Seated on a threadbare rug spread across the earthen floor, Ghulam would recount tales of Kashmir's struggle for autonomy, painting vivid pictures of heroes and martyrs, betrayals and acts of courage. Sameer listened intently, his mind a sponge absorbing every word and every nuance of emotion etched on Ghulam's face.

Under Ghulam's tutelage, Sameer learned about their struggle for *azaadi*[42]—a distorted concept that indoctrinated the youth to take up arms. He absorbed stories of *zulm*[43]— of the supposed atrocities and betrayals that scarred their community. In Sameer's fragile state, Ghulam Bhat proved adept at manipulating his vulnerabilities, pushing him further along a path of destruction with no apparent route of return. He painted a seductive picture of camaraderie and purpose within the militant ranks, where Sameer could find the belonging and significance that had eluded him in his tumultuous home life. As the weeks turned into months, Sameer's visits to Ghulam's hut became more frequent. He skipped school and his textbooks gathered dust on a forgotten shelf as he immersed himself in Ghulam's teachings. Their

---

[42] Freedom.

[43] Torture.

discussions grew more fervent, their plans more daring. Ghulam, sensing Sameer's eagerness to prove himself, introduced him to other young men who shared their vision of azaadi.

With each interaction, Ghulam deepened Sameer's belief that violence and force were the only means to exert influence and carve a place for yourself in the world. He fed Sameer's growing resentment and wish for payback, fuelling the flames of rage that had been building inside him since he was a child. Ghulam's words became a potent catalyst, igniting Sameer's conviction that his destiny lay in aligning with those who wielded power through intimidation and force. Of course, Ghulam Bhat excelled at his task, but could Sameer be blamed? He had neither a father to guide nor a mother to lovingly teach him the difference between right and wrong. Sameer did have a house but not a home; parents but no love; and a family but no sense of belonging. Even the gentle touch of his mother's hand on his head was a distant memory for Sameer, buried beneath the weight of frustration and fear.

One afternoon, as Sameer trudged along the dusty path to Ghulam Bhat's hut, he passed by a view that stirred a longing deep within him. A woman draped in a vibrant orange phiran adorned with delicate needlework sat on the doorstep of her humble home. Wrapped in her arms, nestled against her chest, was her son—perhaps no older than Sameer himself. The affectionate display unfolded before him, bathed in the soft glow of the afternoon sun. Sameer paused; his eyes fixed on this unfamiliar display of maternal warmth. He watched as the woman lovingly fed the son, their bond palpable in the simple act of nourishment and care. The sight pierced through Sameer's hardened exterior, stirring a tumult of emotions that he struggled to articulate. For a fleeting moment, Sameer yearned to trade places with that child, to experience the embrace of a mother's love and the soothing sound of her voice. But the fantasy dissolved as quickly as it had formed, leaving behind an ache that resonated deep within Sameer's soul.

As he approached Ghulam Bhat's modest abode, Sameer's steps faltered. He hesitated as the weight of his own vulnerability pressed upon him. The image of that mother and child lingered in his mind, as a stark reminder of what he had been denied. He longed to escape the harsh realities of his existence, and to find solace in the stories and promises that Ghulam Bhat offered. Ghulam Bhat's hypnotic words were Sameer's escape from reality.

Ghulam Bhat greeted Sameer in the dimly lit room with a knowing smile that spoke volumes of their understanding and how Sameer shouldn't feel alone in his presence. A man that good at manipulation, could make fiction pass off as fact. '*Aao Sameer baitho, aaj der ho gayi*' (Come, Sameer, sit, but what took you so long today?), Ghulam beckoned, his voice a soothing balm to Sameer's troubled spirit. Sameer then broached a request that bore the weight of vulnerability he seldom revealed, '*Kya mein aapki gode mein sarr rakh ke baatein sun sakta hun?*' (Can I…. Can I rest my head on your lap while you tell me stories?). His voice trembled with a rawness that startled even Sameer himself.

Ghulam Bhat, the shrewd manipulator that he was, sensed an opportunity to solidify his influence over the impressionable boy. With a sly smile, he gestured for Sameer to sit beside him. '*Kyun nahi. Aajao. Ab tum parivar ka hissa ho*' (Of course, my boy. You're family now. Come, rest your head here and listen to tales that will open your eyes to the world beyond these valleys). Sameer complied, his head finding a tentative resting place on Ghulam's lap. He closed his eyes, seeking comfort in the imagined warmth of a nurturing presence, but found only the coarse fabric of Ghulam's worn phiran beneath his cheek. In that intimate moment, as Ghulam's voice wove tales of bravery and righteousness, Sameer's troubled heart yearned for the elusive embrace of maternal affection that threatened to anchor him deeper into Ghulam's web of influence and deception.

Ghulam began in a low, hypnotic tone, weaving stories of a cause that he portrayed to be greater than oneself. '*Dekho Sameer, hum sab ek khel aksar khelte hain jiska naam hai journey to paradise*' (You see, Sameer, there's a game we play here—journey to paradise), Ghulam murmured, his voice like a velvet thread winding through Sameer's troubled thoughts. '*Paradise pahunchne ke liye, humein uske kaabil saabit hona hota hai. Kayi levels hote hain; video games mein jaise hota hai. Levels iss type ke hote hain: dushman par fire karna, jo humari awaaz daba rahe hain unhe yahan aane se rokne ke liye pathar baazi karna, aur kayi saare levels*' (To reach paradise, one must prove oneself worthy of it. It starts with simple tasks, like firing at the enemy to protect our honour and pelting stones at those who seek to oppress us).

In Ghulam's narrative, this 'game' unfolded like a twisted pilgrimage, with each level representing a test of loyalty and courage. The first level beckoned with promises of respect and admiration amongst peers. '*Hum mein shahmil hone ke liye, tumhe dikhana padega ki humari iss ladai mein tum daroge nahin'* (To join our ranks, Sameer, you must show you're not afraid to defend what's right), Ghulam continued. His words painted a compelling picture of belonging and purpose for Sameer in a world that had thus far denied him both. They spoke to his desire for agency; for a path out of the shadows cast by his father's violence and his mother's silent resignation. Yet beneath the surface of Ghulam's enticing promises lay a dark truth—one that Sameer, in his desperation, was oblivious to. The journey to paradise was not just a game; it was a seductive trap designed to ensnare vulnerable souls like his own in a web of violence and manipulation.

Sameer's emotions churned like a tempest within him as he walked home. As the night deepened, the air thickened with the weight of Ghulam's influence, drawing him further into the tornado of fervent ideology and false promises. As Ghulam described it, the journey to paradise became a captivating pathway for Sameer.

The following day unfolded with Sameer shouldering a bag heavy with books that would remain carefully arranged and untouched till the end of the day as he trod the familiar path to Ghulam Bhat's humble abode. Sameer's routine had become quite familiar yet unsettlingly repetitive as Ghulam Bhat's stories had become deeply ingrained in Sameer's mind, pulling at him like an invisible force guiding him towards the man who captivated his curiosity and won his trust. Entering his hut, Sameer found the atmosphere subtly altered. Ghulam, usually a font of sagacious anecdotes and historical recollections, greeted Sameer with a gaze that seemed to penetrate to the core of Sameer's being. There was an intensity in his demeanour that piqued Sameer's curiosity, setting the stage for what would unfold next. As Sameer settled himself on a threadbare cushion, Ghulam posed a question that hung heavy with meaning: '*Dushman kon hai?*' (Who is a nemesis?) Sameer, caught off guard by the philosophical depth of the inquiry, hesitated for a brief moment before blurting out the first name that came to his mind. 'Kesar Majid.' Ghulam Bhat's reaction was immediate yet measured, his surprise thinly veiled behind a mask of contemplation. '*Aur bataiye*' (Tell me more), he prompted. His voice underscored a quiet command as he was intrigued to hear a name while most other recruits would be giving definitions. And so, with a blend of raw, lonely and justifiable rage, Sameer recounted the tale of his father's indebtedness to Kesar Majid—a man whose wealth and influence knew no bounds in the village. Sameer described one harsh winter a few years ago when the roof of their house had succumbed to the weight of the snow, forcing his father to seek financial assistance from Kesar Majid. Kesar Majid had initially extended a helping hand, but soon after, a delay in repayment transformed his attitude into one of scorn and contempt. Sameer vividly recalled the day when Kesar Majid had subjected his father to harsh words in front of the village panchayat and stained his honour. Kesar Majid's words had cut more profound than any physical blow.

That day, Sameer confessed with a quiet intensity, '*Maine kasam khayi thi, Abu ki bezatti ka badla lena hai. Uss din Kesar Majid mera dushman ban gaya tha*' (I swore to avenge my father's humiliation. That day, Kesar Majid became my enemy). Hearing Sameer's declaration, Ghulam Bhat's wrinkled face broke into a crooked smile. Rising slowly from his seat, Ghulam Bhat approached a weather-beaten iron box nestled in the corner. He then unlatched the rusted lid, revealing a small, bleached black bag secured with a buckle. The aged leather creaked as Ghulam Bhat lifted the bag from its resting place, the weight of its contents palpable even before he extended it towards Sameer. Ghulam then relinquished the bag into Sameer's outstretched hands. *'Pehli stage shuru'* (First stage begins now), Ghulam Bhat spoke with a gravity that matched the weight of the moment. *'Apna badla lo aur wapas aao'* (Take your revenge and come back to me).

The bag felt heavy with purpose as Sameer took hold of it; the reality of his mission settling upon him like a weighing cloak. As he cautiously reached into the bag, his fingers brushed against the cool, smooth surface of something unfamiliar. Sameer carefully withdrew the object from the black bag. He curled his fingers around the firm grip of the pistol. Surprisingly, there was no tremor in his hands; instead, a sense of eerie familiarity settled over him as if he had held such a weapon countless times before. Gazing at the gun, he felt a mix of awe and trepidation. This was more than just a weapon; it symbolized authority, power and the capacity to enact change. It represented a departure from his childhood innocence, thrusting him into the harsh realities of adulthood.

That night, in the small, dimly lit room he shared with his family, Sameer lay awake, the gun tucked securely under his pillow. His thoughts churned with a mix of anxiety and determination. The weapon's presence so close to him felt daunting yet empowering. As he lay in bed, the stillness of the night enveloped him like a ghost. His mind, restless and consumed by thoughts of vengeance against Kesar

Majid, grappled with the enormity of choices he possessed to eliminate his nemesis. While his mind wandered astray, Sameer absentmindedly traced the contours of the gun hidden under his pillow, a constant reminder of the power he now possessed. Each scenario that he envisioned to eliminate Kesar Majid felt like a chess move in a high-stakes game where every decision could lead to victory or catastrophe.

The following day, as the sun slowly descended behind the rugged mountains, Sameer stood discreetly across the road from Kesar Majid's cyber cafe. The day was winding down, and the village hummed with the sounds of shopkeepers closing up after a day's hard work. Inside the cafe, Kesar Majid meticulously tallied his earnings; his brow furrowed in concentration as he prepared to shut the shop for the night. Sameer, his features obscured by a steel grey cloth wrapped tightly around his face, watched intently from his vantage point. His eyes fixed unwaveringly on his target as his mind erupted in determination and simmering rage.

Memories of the insults hurled at his father flooded Sameer's mind, fuelling the fire within him as he took measured steps forward. His heart pounded in his chest like a steady rhythm of anticipation and nerves as he closed the distance between himself and his target. With every stride, the gravity of what he was about to do weighed heavily on him, yet he felt strangely liberated by the clarity of his mission.

As he neared the entrance of the cyber cafe, Sameer's grip tightened around the cold metal of his gun. With a swift and relentless motion, he raised his gun and aimed with practised precision at Kesar Majid, who was still engrossed in caring for his day's earnings, oblivious to the impending tragedy. In an instant that seemed both fleeting and eternal, the sound of a single gunshot shattered the evening calm, ringing through the village square with a startling intensity. Sameer's heart skipped a beat as the noise of the gunshot reverberated in his ears—a stark reminder of the irreversible nature of his actions. For a brief moment, he stood frozen in time, as the weight of what he had done settled in his bones like an unshakable burden.

Amidst the shock and turmoil, Sameer's instincts kicked in. With adrenaline coursing through his veins, he sprang into action. His footsteps pounded against the earth, stirring up clouds of dust as he raced towards Ghulam Bhat's residence. In a heartbeat, everything had changed for the sixteen-year-old boy. He had sealed his fate when he pulled the trigger, and there was no going back. The warmth he yearned for, the normal life he once knew, all vanished in an instant. Ghulam Bhat's influence twisted Sameer's innocence, leaving him trapped in a life he could never imagine. It is heartbreaking how easily a fragile mind could be led astray, enticed by a dangerous 'game' that promised power but delivered only tragedy. Sameer's story, though just begun, is a stark reminder of the devastating impact of manipulation on young hearts and minds and the irreversible consequences that follow.

As Sameer approached Ghulam Bhat's door, with his chest heaving and heart pounding, he knew that he had set in motion a chain of events that would shape his destiny in ways he could never have foreseen. Sameer's knuckles rapped urgently on Ghulam Bhat's old wooden door, as sweat dripped from his face and tears of fear and triumph blurred his vision. When the door creaked open, revealing Ghulam

Bhat's startled face, Sameer rushed in immediately and locked the door behind him. '*Maine.. maine kar diya. Dushman khatam*' (I... I've done it! The enemy has been eliminated), Sameer gasped, each word was a laborious exhalation as he collapsed on the floor with his back placed against the rough-hewn wall of the hut.

Ghulam Bhat's eyes widened in disbelief, tempered with a grudging respect for the boy who had surpassed his expectations. Sameer wasn't the first recruit he had groomed, but he was the first to eliminate his target with such precision and speed. He couldn't help but marvel at Sameer's natural flair for violence. '*Ab yahan rehna tumhare liye mehfooz nahi hai*' (It's not safe for you here anymore), Ghulam Bhat continued, his tone now urgent. '*Afzal tumhe group headquarter le jayega. Ghar lautne ke baare mein sochna bhi mat. Tum kaafi aage aa chuke ho*' (Afzal will escort you to the group headquarters. Don't even think of returning home. You're in too deep now).

Sameer's world seemed to spin. He hadn't even said a proper goodbye to his family or taken one last look at his mother. The familiar comforts of his family home—the scent of his mother's cooking and his sister's laughter—now felt like distant memories slipping through his fingers. Life for him had changed in an instant. Yet, despite the heaviness in his chest, Sameer felt an unfamiliar sense of accomplishment—a feeling he had never known before from either when he scored the highest marks in his class or when his team would win a cricket match. It indeed was a dangerous rush. His hands, which had once held schoolbooks and cricket bats, now gripped a weapon that symbolized not just power but the irreversible course of his fate. As Sameer walked away from

Ghulam Bhat's hut, the weight of his decision settled heavily upon his young shoulders. His mind replayed Ghulam Bhat's words like an ominous mantra as he navigated the dusty path in his village. The houses that lined the path appeared as darkened shapes; their windows glinting with the last gleams of sunlight. Even the dogs barking in the distance felt as if their voices were carrying a warning that kept ringing in Sameer's unsettled mind. His thoughts swirled with conflicting emotion as the fear of the unknown mingled with a strange anticipation for what lay ahead. The gun tucked beneath his jacket felt heavier than ever—its presence both reassured and terrified him.

Afzal awaited him at the edge of the village, a figure silhouetted against the backdrop of the darkening sky. Sameer's footsteps faltered for a moment as he approached; his mind swirling with doubts and fears. Would he ever see his family again? Could he truly leave behind the warmth and familiarity of his village? Would he ever be able to hear the laughter of his sisters? Sameer took a deep breath as his throat became dry with nerves. He glanced back at the village one last time, the place that had been his home, his life. Memories of his family flashed through his mind.

But in the middle of the ache of nostalgia, a newfound resolve stirred within Sameer's heart. He was no longer just Sameer Ahmad Bhat. He had become something more, at least in his head—a warrior in a world where courage and sacrifice were currency. With a firm resolve, Sameer's eyes met Afzal, and he followed him into the unknown. As he disappeared into the dense thicket of Tral, Sameer knew that there was no turning back. The path ahead was indeed uncertain and fraught with danger, yet Sameer walked forward with a thirst for belonging.

One might think this was the end of Sameer's story, but it was only the beginning of a new chapter. That day, Sameer Ahmad Bhat ceased to exist, and from the ashes emerged SAMEER TIGER—a name that would be synonymous with fear and brutality throughout the valley of Kashmir.

# #9

# The Viral Video:
# A Threat or an Opportunity?

In the serene valleys of Kashmir, where the mountains stand as quiet custodians and the rivers sing age-old songs, children bear the burden of a conflict not of their making. Innocence, as fragile as the morning dew on delicate petals, is stripped away by forces they never will understand. People like Ghulam Bhat and others like him weave tales of purpose and belonging, entangling the young minds in a web of false promises that ultimately drags them away from the laughter of their playgrounds and closer to the gloom of unrest. What fault lies in their eager hearts? Their only desire is to chase fleeting joys like playing hide-and-seek among the orchards and lazing beneath the shade of majestic trees. They bear no responsibility for the conflict that casts its shadows over their lives, yet they carry its weight in every hesitant step and innocent glance.

The news of Sameer's disappearance raced through the narrow lanes of Drabgam. Every corner of the village was filled with the worried voices of his parents, who tirelessly questioned every soul and searched every nook and cranny for their son. Their anguish knew no bounds as they frantically moved through every street looking for their son. With all avenues seemingly closed, they turned to the police station. With a scared heart and a heavy head, they filed a missing person report for Sameer. Inside the pale walls of the station, the Station House Officer (SHO), a seasoned police official, was well aware of the unrest in Kashmir and how young children were indoctrinated by militant organizations. He listened gravely as Sameer's parents poured out their fears. The phenomenon of youths slipping away to join militant ranks was tragically familiar. Their names were recorded in the ominous 'red book' of suspected militants. As the SHO meticulously documented their anguish, he couldn't shake the coincidence that on the very night that Sameer disappeared, Kesar Majid met his unfortunate end.

As the family nervously awaited their son's return, Sameer slipped into the folds of Hizbul Mujahideen, like a river merging silently with the turbulent sea, where each ripple of his presence expanded the currents of insurgency in Kashmir. His transformation from an ordinary youth to a pivotal figure within the militant group was swift and seamless. To the outside world, he remained a shadow as his identity was concealed behind the veil of secrecy that obscured their operations. But within the folds of Hizbul Mujahideen, Sameer flourished. His initiation into the ranks marked the beginning of a meteoric rise. His determination and strategic acumen quickly caught the eye of his senior leaders. Before long, he assumed the role of a recruiter, wielding words that resonated deeply with the disillusioned youth across the region. Sameer spoke of 'jannat'—the paradise that awaited those who fought for their cause and 'azaadi'—the elusive freedom that had become synonymous with their struggle.

It wasn't long ago that Ghulam Bhat recruited Sameer into the circle of Hizbul Mujahideen. Now, Sameer stood as a prominent figure, drawing young people from Kashmir into the militant group. It's a troubling cycle where those who feel powerless are persuaded to join, only to, in turn, recruit others. This pattern repeats itself; each new recruit is both a victim and a promoter of conflict. Sameer's transformation from a recruit to a recruiter vividly demonstrates the powerful attraction and inherent risks of this path. As this cycle persists, one must ponder: how much longer will it grip Kashmir's youth, fuelling the ongoing violence and unrest?

Under Sameer's guidance, Hizbul Mujahideen embraced new tactics. He introduced the revolutionary idea of using social media to connect their followers, transforming isolated pockets of dissent in different parts of the valley into a formidable digital network. Whenever a comrade of their own would get cornered by the security forces, Sameer's command would spread swiftly through the digital web. Within moments, supporters and sympathizers would mobilize, converging on the scene with stones in their hands. They would then hurl stones at the military personnel, causing chaos and disrupting their ongoing cordon and search operation. This guerilla tactic not only thwarted the authorities but also bought crucial time for the comrades to slip away.

Sameer Tiger, as he came to be known, became more than a leader; he embodied the aspirations of a generation and earned the title 'tiger' for his fearlessness. Notorious for openly challenging military forces and orchestrating operations across the valley, Sameer's unwavering courage and readiness to confront adversity made him popular in his outfit. His influence snowballed rather rapidly and he became a symbol of resistance for the youth, a modern-day messiah offering hope in the face of perceived oppression. Sameer Tiger's legend grew in the convoluted streets of Kashmir's towns and the remote valleys in the countryside. However, people didn't have a face to attach to the name as he was like a phantom that moved like the wind and caused massive destruction. His strategy was meticulous, his vision unfaltering. He navigated the complex terrain of insurgency with a blend of courage and cunning, always one step ahead of those who sought to silence their movement. He was not just a commander but a strategist, weaving a web of resistance that stretched beyond physical barriers. Sameer believed that each stone thrown was not merely an act of defiance but a declaration of identity; a stepping stone in the path to what they deemed rightful independence.

As months passed and Sameer Tiger's influence deepened, so did the intensity of their struggle. His followers embraced his vision with unwavering loyalty, driven by a promise of a future where their voices would no longer be drowned out by the clatter of boots and the rattle of rifles. For Sameer Tiger, his journey was not just a personal odyssey but a collective saga, written in the blood and sweat of those who dared to dream of a future where freedom was more than just a word—it was a reality waiting to be seized. Month after month, Sameer persisted in his audacious stone-pelting assaults on security personnel and their vehicles. With his face perpetually masked but his resolve as solid as mountain rock, his followers mirrored his actions with unflinching loyalty.

Meanwhile, a new figure began to gain prominence in the valley—former member of legislative assembly, Syed Bashir Durrani, a staunch advocate for pro-India sentiments. Syed Bashir Durrani often sang praises of Operation Sadhbhavana[44] as an ardent supporter of the Indian Armed Forces. For Sameer Tiger, Syed Bashir Durrani became a marked target. One fateful dawn, whispers reached Sameer's ears of Durrani's planned visit to Gulshanabad, a sleepy village nestled within the serpentine alleys of Shadimarg Block in Pulwama district. Sameer knew the time had come. Under the veil of darkness, Sameer and his comrades converged on Durrani's temporary refuge, where even the moon, camouflaged under the overcast sky, couldn't testify to the brutality that was about to break loose in the bylanes of Gulshanabad. The wheels of fate began to turn for Syed Bashir Durrani as Sameer Tiger and his men approached his tranquil abode. Like shadows, they infiltrated the house. Inside, the silence was shattered by the sudden eruption of gunfire, echoing like thunderclaps in the stillness. In mere moments, a peaceful household with the

---

[44] Operation Sadbhavana is an initiative by the Indian Army aimed at fostering goodwill and development in Jammu & Kashmir and Ladakh. Its focus is on addressing the needs of people affected by terrorism and insurgency, primarily sponsored by Pakistan. The initiative includes various welfare activities like health care camps, educational initiatives, vocational training programs and infrastructure development projects in the region. Its goal is to win the hearts and minds of the local population, offering them opportunities for a better future and countering the influence of militant groups like Hizbul Mujahideen, Lashkar and Jaish-e-Mohammed, to name a few.

occupants asleep in their rooms transformed into a harrowing battlefield. Bodies fell like autumn leaves in a storm, their lifeblood staining the floor like crimson brushstrokes on the canvas of terror.

The news of the relentless gunfire reached the Shadimarg Company of 44 Rashtriya Rifles through an informant. Their response was swift and determined as the wheels of their vehicle rolled over the rugged terrain with urgency. The night resounded with the ominous rumble of engines and the rhythmic thud of boots on the ground as soldiers raced against time to confront the unfolding tragedy. Amidst the chaotic scene inside Syed Bashir Durrani's home, Sameer retrieved a smartphone and began recording. He captured the brutality on video—with his face concealed, he stood in the middle of wreckage like a dark omen. Through the video, Sameer issued a chilling warning to anyone who dared to harbour pro-India sentiments. His voice pierced the eerie silence; his words, stark and threatening, contrasted sharply with the broken glass and lifeless bodies around him. '*Jihad ke khilaaf bolne ka yehi anjaam hai. Hindustan se jo haath milaega uska yehi ant hoga*' (Speaking against Jihad will make you meet a similar fate. Any pro-India sympathies will lead to a disastrous end), he declared firmly. The camera captured the aftermath—rooms transformed into scenes of violence, with blood staining everyday objects. Each word spoken carried Sameer's unwavering resolve and brutality. His message wasn't just a threat; it promised consequences for Gulshanabad and beyond.

In a matter of minutes, as Aurangzeb and his soldiers arrived, Sameer Tiger vanished into the darkness, leaving behind a scene of unimaginable horror and devastation. Aurangzeb was appalled looking at the bloodshed and the barbarity inflicted by the militants. Bodies lay motionless; even children were not spared. Who would have caused such a havoc? Aurangzeb wondered as they moved the bodies out of the debris of broken furniture. A while later, social media exploded into a frenzy when Sameer Tiger uploaded the video that he had recorded from the site of brutality on the official page of Hizbul Mujahideen through a secure network. The video, though shaky and raw, sent shockwaves across platforms. When it reached 44 Rashtriya rifles, the soldiers were enraged. Aurangzeb immediately rushed to his Company Commander. '*Saab, yeh vohi hai jisne ek hafte pehle humare convoy pe attack kara tha*' (Sir, he is the same person who had attacked our convoy a week ago), Aurangzeb kept pausing the video. '*Tum itne sure kaise ho? Iski toh shakal bhi nahi dikh rahi aur naa hi uss din attack mein militant ki shakal dikhi thi*' (How are you so sure? His face is concealed, and even that day, the attacker's face was covered), the Company Commander asked while looking at the screen. '*Uski aankhein . . . inhe main nahi bhool sakta. Iski aankhon mein itni nafrat, itna gussa aur itna ghamand dikhta hai jo maine uss din bhi dekha tha. Sir, yeh vohi hai*' (His eyes . . . I can't forget his eyes. They are filled with so much hate, anger and arrogance. I saw the same the other day as well). It was then established in Aurangzeb's mind that the two people were, in fact, the same person. But who was he? An unknown man who was bringing everyone to their knees. Before the search party could reach any location, this man, without a face, would mobilize the crowd and create chaos in a matter of minutes.

While everyone in the company tried to join the dots, another notification came up on everyone's screen. This time, a photograph was uploaded—a young boy wearing a blue denim jacket and a black bandana. He had the same deep-seated eyes filled with arrogance as he carried the US-made M-4 Carbine rifle—Sameer Tiger was finally introduced to the world. He made his identity known so that the youth sitting far away could relate to him and idolize him. He wasn't wrong, as his photo and video garnered tremendous support and traction with the comments sections filled with messages about jihad, azaadi and, shockingly, requests to join Sameer in his battle. Sameer Tiger had officially become the poster boy of Kashmiri liberation as he filled the chasm that was created after the death of Burhan Wani.

Weeks passed, and the hunt for this notorious new leader, Sameer Tiger, was on. Every information was acted upon, and every sympathizer was questioned. One fine day, a piece of intelligence information found the soldiers of 44 Rashtriya Rifles on the edge. They learned that Sameer would be visiting his village soon as his sister was getting married in two weeks. The intelligence was specific yet frustratingly vague—Sameer's exact arrival date remained unknown. All they knew was that the stakes were high. Sameer was no ordinary militant on the wanted list. He was the man who had wreaked havoc, killed innocent people and left behind a trail of devastation. He was the one who had been sowing the seeds of dissent in the minds of the local youth. The soldiers had to strike a balance here as they couldn't afford to act hastily, risking tipping off Sameer. This was their chance to put an end to his brutality, and they couldn't let it slip. The informers were put on high alert; any suspicious movement was to be reported and investigated.

The air was tense as Aurangzeb anticipated the arrival of Sameer any time. He knew that they could spring into an operation at the moment, and it wouldn't be an easy one. A man this cruel wouldn't give up that easily. That evening, Aurangzeb sat in his company, staring at the setting sun. He captured the moment on his phone and sent the picture of the setting sun to Ilham with the caption: *'Aaj sunset kaafi sundar hai'* (the sunset is strikingly beautiful today). Instantly, Ilham sent him a picture of the setting sun from Salani and wrote: *'Kya yeh same hai? Mujhe tumhare saath wala sunset chahiye'* (Is it the same? I want the sunset where you are next to me). This was their thing. Every other day, Aurangzeb and Ilham would share pictures of the setting sun with each other. It was their love language; a language without words but with deeper emotions, where distance is immaterial and love triumphs. Through these pictures, Aurangzeb felt as if he was sharing a part of his world with Ilham—a world not bereft of challenges but also one with moments of breathtaking beauty. Aurangzeb and Ilham continued exchanging pictures and heartfelt messages like a routine, expressing their deep longing towards each other despite the miles between them. Each photo that Aurangzeb sent carried a piece of his heart, a silent plea for their love to bridge the distance. In response, Ilham always replied with her own captures of the setting sun, where each image was a poetic declaration of their bond and a dream of a future together. With every exchange of these captured moments and sweet nothings, their love blossomed. The sunset became a symbol of their love story—a reminder that even in life's challenges, there is always room for beauty and hope. Of course, while Aurangzeb found himself getting closer to Ilham with each passing day, the thought that someday, any bullet could end their story would cross his mind, now more often than ever with this notorious militant roaming the streets of Kashmir scot-free.

There was no news of Sameer for the next few days, but it was the lull before the storm. The self-proclaimed 'tiger' would, of course, try to roar. And as anticipated, he roared a little out of line this time. Sameer Tiger released a video; it wasn't an ordinary video but a direct threat to the Company Commander and soldiers of the Shadimarg company of 44 Rashtriya Rifles. Sat with unabashed pride and self-importance, he uttered the words that changed his world—'*44 RR ke company commander se bolna ki sher ne shikar karna kya chodh diya, kutton ne samjha jungle unka hai. Usse bolna ki maa ka doodh piya hai toh saamne aaye*' (Tell the Company Commander of 44 RR that just because the tiger stopped hunting, dogs thought they ruled the land. Tell him that if they have the guts, they should come to see me eye to eye). He thought he had hit the nail with this video and would be revered across the land for his guts and courage. Love outpoured for Sameer in a matter of minutes, and people commented stuff as absurd as, '*Itni himmat wala humara pradhan mantri hona chahiye*' (A man with such courage should be our Prime Minister). What no one knew then was that Sameer's life was about to change.

The situation in 44 Rashtriya Rifles Shadimarg company was tense as every soldier clenched their fists, replaying the video again and again. Sameer Tiger's words reignited the simmering anger in their hearts as they remembered the villages scarred by violence and lives shattered by fear. For the soldiers, if their Company Commander received a direct threat from a militant, it was also a blow to them. His presence commanded respect, not just for his rank, but for how he inspired camaraderie among his troops. With every mission, he mapped out strategies like a captain charting a course, balancing tactical precision with a deep understanding of the terrain and the enemy's moves.

Aurangzeb was particularly irked as he was very emotionally attached to the Company Commander. He kept playing the video like a stuck record. Something was amiss. He was surely missing some detail. It was then that Aurangzeb's eyes widened; he paused the video and zoomed in to focus on the background. It was a pale wall, but it had some sort of symbol debossed on one side of it. He had seen this symbol before. Aurangzeb jogged his memory for a moment and rushed, '*Sir, sir, yeh vohi symbol hai jo Kashmir mein jo auratein overground worker ka kaam kar rahi hain apne kisi family member ki death ke baad. Voh kayi kone mein yeh banati hain unity dikhane ke liye*' (Sir, sir, this is the same symbol that a lot of women who become overground workers after the death of someone dear in Kashmir deboss on their walls as a symbol of solidarity). Aurangzeb had seen this symbol a few months ago during one of his covert operations—two vertical lines with a crescent moon, a star in the middle and 'Allah' written on top in Urdu. He knew it was the same symbol. As per their records of the area, there was only one house in the village, which belonged to Gufrana Begum, an overground worker who had fled the village a few years ago. The house was now abandoned, and Sameer couldn't have imagined a better hideout.

The Company Commander gave swift commands through crackling radios, ordering his soldiers to scramble into action. The soldiers split up into teams and rushed. Their boots kicked up dust as they fanned out and encircled the village. The periphery cordon was tightened to ensure that Sameer Tiger had no avenue for escape.

Meanwhile, in the stillness of a neighbouring house, seven young girls sat cross-legged on the floor, engrossed in their Quran lessons with their gentle teacher, oblivious to the chaos outside. The sudden arrival of armed soldiers disrupted their afternoon ritual. The soldiers had to ensure that all houses near the target house were vacated to avoid any collateral civilian casualties. Aurangzeb entered the house respectfully, and, in his calm yet urgent voice, guided the children out to safety, far away from the impending storm.

Inside Sameer's hideout, tension coiled like a tightly wound spring. Sameer, a figure fuelled by the adrenaline of rebellion and the echoes of past victories, was caught off guard. The news that the Indian Army had swiftly pinpointed his location, less than twenty-four hours after his provocative video, sent shockwaves through his psyche. He found it challenging to comprehend the events unfolding beyond the walls of his hideout. The intensity of the situation was surreal. Sameer's mind raced. His thoughts, usually sharp and calculating, now whirled in disbelief. How could they have found him so quickly? Yet, his ego, as towering as the mountains surrounding the village, refused to concede defeat so easily. Surrender wasn't in Sameer's vocabulary. The idea of kneeling before the forces he had fought against for years was unthinkable. While huddled in his hideout, the cacophony of gunfire outside grew louder, echoing through the cramped space. Sameer's thoughts raced back to the beginning. Years ago, he had abandoned his family to follow this path. He hadn't given up everything to fall on his knees one day before the military forces. He was a role model for the disillusioned youth, and he could give up limbs but could not give up arms. In the tense silence between the gunshots, Sameer's mind raced against the clock. The idea that there was a possibility of getting captured pushed him to think faster and act quicker. With a sharp jerk to his head, he snapped back to the grim reality closing in around him. When he couldn't find any route to escape, he called Aslam and asked him to gather sympathizers in Drabgam as the security forces had sealed all exit routes and were closing in on him.

After the call, Sameer tightened his grip on the weapon and unleashed a torrent of bullets through the crevices and the shattered window pane. The soldiers outside were taken by surprise as they rushed to take cover, retaliating in measured bursts to avoid any casualty on their side.

The standoff intensified as hours passed, with Sameer steadfastly holding his ground and the soldiers continuing to maintain a tight perimeter. Aurangzeb ducked and reached the Company Commander to inform him that Sameer would never give up arms and walk out. He might be orchestrating an escape route by using his own guerilla tactics. Before the village drowned under a sea of angry faces hurling stones at the security personnel, they had to eliminate Sameer. The Company Commander ordered Aurangzeb to call for the water bowser filled with petrol. Aurangzeb followed his orders swiftly and directed the nozzle pipe's force to douse the entire house with petrol. The pungent scent of fuel saturated the air of Drabgam and added an ominous tension to the scene. With a steady hand, they set the house ablaze. In a matter of seconds, flames erupted at the scene, licking at the dry timber and cloth that lined Sameer's hideout. The crackling roar of fire drowned out the earlier gunfire, casting dancing shadows that painted the village walls with flickering orange hues. It was a scene to witness—soldiers with their fingers placed on the trigger, taking cover around the house, and a ginormous bonfire of a house erupting in front of their eyes. As the inferno engulfed the structure, tension mounted among the soldiers. They watched intently; their eyes fixed on the target as they anticipated Sameer's response to the blaze that threatened to consume his hideout. Eagerly stationed, the soldiers awaited Sameer's next move.

Inside the hideout, Sameer couldn't wrap his head around what was happening. He thought he would shoot down a few soldiers till his supporters arrived, and then, in the mad chaos, slip away. But the Indian Army had planned a better farewell for him. Sameer felt the heat closing in as his steps kept receding from the fire. The smoke made his eyes sting and blurred his vision, but he aimlessly kept firing shots like a tornado. As the fire raged on, consuming everything in its path, Sameer faced a critical decision. With each passing moment, the pressure mounted for him. Should he stay inside and risk being burnt to flames, or should he step out and brave the uncertainty beyond the walls? It was when his lungs started choking that he rushed up the wooden staircase for air.

In the mayhem, Aurangzeb maintained his vigil. While everybody was expecting Sameer to walk out of the front door with his arms raised, Aurangzeb's trained instincts urged him to keep his aim steady, not towards the expected front door exit where Sameer might surrender, but towards the roof. His eyes scanned through the smoke and flames, searching for any movement on the roof. It was a tricky situation because if Sameer managed to escape that day, they would never be able to curtail his brutality. At that very moment, Sameer, with adrenaline-infused agility, sprang on the roof and hailed bullets at the soldiers below. He was hoping to escape the tense noose, but Aurangzeb, with his razor-sharp instinct, was ready to welcome him. The moment Sameer set foot on the roof, a piercing bullet passed through the centre of his forehead, and in the blink of an eye, Sameer was dead.

A man so brutal, barbaric and merciless was brought to his knees less than twenty-four hours after he threatened the Indian Army. His encounter served as a direct warning to all the radical nefarious elements spread across the valley that their time in India was over. There was no mercy for killing the innocent, joining hands with neighbours or harbouring feelings of dissent. However glorious the chapters of Sameer Tiger's life looked like, he had died a meagre death.

The news of Sameer Tiger's death led to mourning in the valley. People in the thousands gathered at Drabgam to bid him farewell. For the sympathizers, they had lost their own—a man who was ready to give his all for their liberation. Nobody cared how many innocent lives he took; all they cared about was how this 'messiah' was now one with God, and the ones left behind had to take his mission forward. Women were howling as if their world had collapsed. Under the debris of indoctrinated minds was a girl who rushed towards his body. All she wanted was to wipe her handkerchief on Sameer's face one last time as his remembrance.

So many soldiers lose their lives in such operations and for no fault of theirs. Sameer Tiger's story should be a reminder that no matter what the childhood trauma or struggle, killing innocent people or taking up arms is never the solution.

The day Sameer joined Hizbul Mujahideen, his parents were dead inside. No respectable man could see his son become a militant; they could no longer walk with their heads high. Were they paying the price for Sameer's deeds? They were, and they will do so for as long as they will live . . .

# #10

# The Abduction

## Army Barracks,
## 13 June 2018

As the sun shifted west, Aurangzeb found himself in the quiet solitude of his barracks. Since childhood, Ramzan[45] was his favourite time of the year—the entire village would come alive with iftari daawats[46] and imam sahib's sermons every Friday. As the muezzin's call to prayer resonated through the valley, memories flooded his mind. Since the time he joined the Indian Army, the month of Ramzan would bring in tart–sweet memories as now he would, of course, pray but not have Ammi blow her duas at him; have dates and water to break his fast but not his siblings fighting for the last piece of gulgula;[47]

---

[45] A holy month of fasting, prayer and community for the Muslims.

[46] A traditional feast or meal that takes place during the month of Ramadan to break the fast after sunset.

[47] A deep-fried sweet made with wheat flour and jaggery.

the dastarkhwan[48] would be laid with his extended family of soldiers seated but not have Ammi's sweet voice calling out to him. How he wished he would be back home surrounded by loved ones instead of this solitary outpost. For everyone else, he was a warrior protecting the nation, but deep down, he was a little boy who just wanted to lay his head on his mother's lap and count the stars. As the time for asr namaz[49] drew near, Aurangzeb moved his black trunk with 'Rifleman Aurangzeb' stencilled in white under the wooden single bed. The beds in the soldiers' barracks are peculiar—they all have four vertical iron rods tied to each end, with the mosquito net neatly folded upwards that would be pulled down before calling it a night. He then began mopping the space between the eggshell-coloured wall and his bed. As per ritual, he then placed his emerald-coloured, mihrab-woven prayer rug on the floor and prepared himself for the evening prayers.

As Aurangzeb descended to pray, kneeling down and facing the direction of Kaaba,[50] the chaos in his mind turned to clarity, and he became one with his creator. He would always be grateful to witness another sunrise, as every bullet dodged because of his mother's prayers would bring him a day closer to home.

After the prayer, his thoughts turned to his family. He longed for his mother's embrace, the comforting scent of her

---

[48] A Persian and Turkish term which means tablecloth or a cloth spread used for layout of food items which is spread on the floor.

[49] One of the five daily prayers of Islam. Asr is usually prayed when the Sun is halfway between noon and sunset.

[50] Direction of the Sacred Mosque in Mecca. It's the direction which all Muslims face when performing their prayers, wherever they are in the world.

cooking filling the air, the laughter of his siblings echoing through the halls of their modest homes and the inspecting eyes of his father looking for traces of soldiering on his body. Here, in the distant land, his wandering mind was brought back to the present by the cacophony of gunfire resounding in the distance. He soon realized that it was time for iftar.[51]

Even in the midst of loneliness and longing, there was a sense of unity that transcended the boundaries of time and space. For even as Aurangzeb broke his fast with a simple meal of dates and water, he knew that hundreds of miles away, his family would be doing the same. In the shared moment of reflection and renewal, they were bound together by the threads of love and devotion that stretched across the vast expanse of their homeland. Day after day, Aurangzeb would be involved in operations around Shopian while continuing his dual duty as a soldier and a god-fearing person. There were times when he would return to his company location after a night-long cordon and search operation, and while everyone else would hit the sack, Aurangzeb would take a shower, offer his *fajr ki namaz*[52] (without *sehri*[53] as the langar would be closed at dawn) and go off to sleep. He believed that one should be grateful to one's creator for being born in this land and should also be devoted to the people of the land.

As Ramzan drew to a close, Aurangzeb's eagerness to visit Salani skyrocketed, but his duty was above everything else.

---

[51] The name of the meal eaten by Muslims at sunset to break their fast during the holy month of Ramadan.

[52] Early morning prayer.

[53] The morning meal eaten by Muslims before the sun has come up during Ramadan.

Even though he would always plan his leave in such a manner as to be home for Eid, this time was different. Militant activities had multiplied manifold in the last few weeks. Though the governments of India and Pakistan had announced a ceasefire agreement during the month of Ramzan, incidents of terror activities would be reported now and then. Aurangzeb wanted to be there as the company would receive intelligence about the location of militants taking refuge in some nearby village every other day. The situation intensified more so after the killing of Sameer Tiger the previous month by Aurangzeb and his company men.

Militant organizations from across the border had been trying to unite the youth of Kashmir ever since Burhan Wani was killed in 2016. Wani, of course, became more influential from his grave than alive as armed rebellion erupted against the Indian Armed forces in the region, with frequent clashes between the local rebels and the security forces. His grave became a memorial for all the young people aspiring for a free Kashmir, and his death gave birth to a new Kashmir with an angry generation ready to face the bullets. But the fire soon fizzled out as the militant groups couldn't find a face to unite the young blood. It was then that Sameer Tiger rose to fame as the poster boy of Kashmiri liberation. With his death, Kashmir once again was enraged by the surge in militancy, fearless youth taking up arms and new cases of abduction or violence being reported every other day.

As the morning unfolded, the atmosphere remained tranquil, with no reports of terrorist activities, allowing soldiers to focus on their routine tasks. Yet, beneath this apparent calm, a sense of foreboding lingered, reminiscent of the eerie stillness before a storm unleashed its fury.

While Aurangzeb stood outside his company barrack, helping Joginder Singh, his fellow soldier, tie his turban, the Company Commander walked past. '*Jai Hind Sahab*', the two soldiers saluted in unison, supplanted by the muezzin's call to prayer in the background. The Company Commander's steps receded immediately. He turned towards Aurangzeb and enquired, '*Jai hind! Aurangzeb Eid kab hai?* (Jai Hind! Aurangzeb, when is Eid?) '*Sahab, 2 din baad*' (Sir, in 2 days), Aurangzeb instantly replied as if he had wanted to say it out loud for quite some time. '*Toh ghar ke itne pass posted ho. Gaon nahi jana kya?*' (You're posted so close to home; don't you wish to visit your village for Eid?) the Company Commander enquired with inquisitive eyes. '*Sahab, Kashmir mein abhi mahaul sahi nahi hai. Company mein he rahunga. Kabhi bhi operation launch ho sakta hai*' (Sir, the environment in Kashmir is quite hostile. I'll stay in my company location only as an operation could be launched anytime), Aurangzeb replied. *Operation? Mahaul toh Kashmir ka badalte mausam jaisa hai, Kabhi garam kabhi thanda. Kuch hoga toh baaki Jawan haina. Tum kuch din ghar jaye aao.* (Operation? The situation in Kashmir is always turbulent and volatile. In case of any untoward situation, other soldiers are there. You go home for two days), the Company Commander ordered. Aurangzeb seemed reluctant initially, but the thought of meeting his mother instantly lifted his spirits. As he moved inside his barrack, his leaps showed subtle enthusiasm. '*Kya ho gaya, itna khush?*' (What happened? How come you're so happy?), Tajamul Ahmad, a fellow soldier, inquired. '*Ammi se milne jaa raha hun, Sahab ne chutti di hai*' (I am going home. Sir has granted me leave).

Aurangzeb then began packing his essentials and made a rather enthusiastic call to his younger brother, Shabbir. '*As-*

*salaam alaikum bhai, kaise ho?* (Hello brother, how are you?), Shabbir would always greet Aurangzeb with love and respect. *'Wa-Alaikum-Salaam, ek khush khabri hai'* (Hello, I have good news), Aurangzeb replied. *'Aap Eid ke liye ghar aa rahe ho kya? Ammi kal se Poonch rahi hain'* (Please tell me you're coming home for Eid. Mother has been enquiring since yesterday), Shabbir's voice echoed with excitement. *'Ammi se kehna kal dopahar ke khane tak ghar par hounga, aur meri pasand ka . . .'*(Yes, tell mother I'll be home by lunchtime tomorrow and ask her to make....) Aurangzeb was interrupted. *'Haan, haan pata hai—safed makhan, shakkar aur makki ki roti tayaar rahegi aapke swagat mein. Jevi bhai iss baar aapne mere liye kaunse rang ke kapde liye hain eid ke liye? Mere jooton se match hone chahiye'* (Yes, yes, I know. White butter, jaggery powder and chickpea bread will be ready for you. Brother, which colour of garment did you purchase for me this time to wear on Eid? I hope it matches my shoes), Shabbir couldn't wait. Aurangzeb slapped his forehead as the thought of purchasing gifts hadn't even crossed his mind. *'Shabbir tum mujhe lene Poonch aa jana aur sabke liye matching kapde vahin se le lenge. Theek hai?'* (Shabbir, you come to Poonch tomorrow to pick me up, and we'll buy matching clothes for everyone from the market there. Is that alright?) Aurangzeb replied, stuffing his clothes in a black rucksack. *'Theek hai bhai. Ammi bahot khush hongi. Kal Qasim bhai bhi pahunch rahe hain. Allah hafiz!'* (Okay, brother. Mother would be delighted to learn that you are coming. Brother Qasim is also coming tomorrow. I shall see you. Bye), Shabbir said.

While Aurangzeb was busy sorting his stuff, his friends in the company volunteered to call a cab so he could be taken to Poonch the following day. Aurangzeb expressed his gratitude. That night, he kept tossing in his sleep as he felt that the hands of the clock were moving at a snail's speed. The next day, he stirred from sleep before sunrise, feeling the first hints of daylight tiptoeing through the crack in the wooden door. Without letting a single minute slip away, Aurangzeb got ready and moved towards the sentry check post. Even the flowers planted on either side of the gravel road looked breathtaking that particular morning. Nothing could spoil Aurangzeb's mood that day as he kept counting the hours left to see family—his younger siblings had taught him the concept of DLTGH (days left to go home) and now he was counting hours.

Aurangzeb stepped out of the company location and turned towards the sentry on duty to bid him goodbye. *'Bhai, sheer korma*[54] *lana mat bhoolna'* (Brother, don't forget to bring sheer korma), the sentry on duty spoke from atop the iron-guarded watchtower. *'Zaroor janab, sabke liye launga'* (Sure, sir. I shall get it for everyone), Aurangzeb waved at the sentry.

That morning, Nazeera Begum's eyes were glued to the massive iron gates of the company location. Every creek would make her jump from her seat at the tea stall. It was as if something was bothering her immensely. Just a day earlier, she had overheard two men conversing about the planned abduction of a military personnel from the area; she thought it could be false but not wanting to take a chance, she had been trying to get in touch with Aurangzeb but had no luck. That day, she opened her stall earlier than usual to be able to share the fresh information with Aurangzeb. In that precise

---

[54] A festival vermicelli pudding prepared by Muslims on Eid ul-Fitr and Eid al-Adha in India.

instant, a Swift Dzire rolled before the company gate. Nazeera Begum immediately realized that the news was, after all, not fake. In tandem with the car coming to a screeching halt, a soldier exited the main guarded gate. The moment she saw the soldier's face, her tea vessel slipped and bounced against the slab with hot tea sprinkling all over. Not even realizing that her forearm had blisters, she rushed towards the vehicle. But before she could call out to him, Aurangzeb boarded the cab and left. Nazeera Begum kneeled on the ground as she screamed—'*Gaadi roko, gaadi roko*' (Stop the car, stop the car). But unfortunately, owing to her age, her scream went unheard.

She began crying on the roadside, clutching her head. A passerby, looking at the old lady in the middle of the road, rushed towards her. '*Appa, kya hua? Sab khariyat?*' (Aunt, what happened? All well?) Nazeera Begum couldn't utter a word as she dried her tears and rose to shut the store before making her way home.

'*Yaar bhai kya naam hai aapka?*' (Brother, what is your name?), Aurangzeb asked the taxi driver as he settled himself on the back left side of the vehicle. 'Sir, Farooq Ahmed,' the driver replied, looking through the rearview mirror. '*Yaar, yeh "sir" wali formality kisi aur ke saath karna. Mujhe tum apna bhai samjho*' (Friend, don't be so formal. Please consider me as your brother). Aurangzeb smiled as he texted Shabbir—ETA 11:30 AM. The phone immediately buzzed. It was Shabbir's reply—'*Roger, janab.*'

As Aurangzeb journeyed home through Kashmir's winding roads, he found himself enchanted by its natural beauty. The landscape seemed to breathe with life with its lush greenery and towering mountains. He rolled down the windows, feeling the cool breeze on his face, with the chirping birds providing the appropriate backdrop score. Navigating through the twisted paths, Aurangzeb's mind drifted towards Ilham. He immediately closed his eyes, drawing a picture of her sculpted face in his mind. Aurangzeb loved Ilham in a yellow salwar kameez and imagined her running towards him with her dupatta swaying to the tunes of the wind.

Aurangzeb's love reverie was hindered by Farooq's low-pitched, gravelly voice. *'Bhaijaan, aapko aitraaz na ho toh Pulwama se ek do sawari le lun? Vapas aane ka kharcha nikal jayega'* (Brother, if you don't mind, can I take a passenger or two from Pulwama? It will compensate for when the vehicle would return empty). The compassionate man that Aurangzeb was, he immediately agreed. *'Par Farooq Miya, gaadi mein jitni jagah hai utni he sawari lena, local bus naa bana dena. Kahin aap khud bonnet pe baithe ho'* (But Farooq, take only as many passengers as the space permits. It shouldn't be such that you are sitting on the vehicle's bonnet), Aurangzeb laughed.

He couldn't wait any longer as his fingers swiftly moved on his phone's screen and dialled Ammi's (mother's) number. After two rings, he heard a 'hello' from the other end. *'Arre Ammi, aapki awaaz aadmi jaisi kab se ho gayi?'* (Mother, since when did your voice become so manly?), Aurangzeb laughed at his own poor joke. It was Zafar. He was getting late to pick up Qasim Bhai from the Meander bus stop and had hurriedly left with ammi's phone by mistake. While Aurangzeb was engrossed in the telephonic conversation, the vehicle halted on the black tarmac adorned by well-endowed apple trees on either side. Four men in dark brown and grey oversized phirans boarded the vehicle from both sides. One person entered the co-driver seat. On the rear side, before Aurangzeb could move, he was wedged between three men, one to his left and two to the right. Aurangzeb looked to the left and instantly to the right, his soldier instinct immediately on high alert. Aurangzeb yelled, '*Gaadi roko! Gaadi roko!* (Stop the car! Stop the car!). But before he could finish, a cloth was shoved into his mouth and the wooden stock of an AK-47 met his forehead, causing him to lose consciousness momentarily. Zafar strained to hear his brother's voice over the fuzzy phone connection. Aurangzeb's urgent command echoed through the handset before the line went dead. Frowning at the silent phone, Zafar remembered Aurangzeb's strict rule—never call back if the line drops. Zafar thought that Aurangzeb must have reached Peer ki Gali peak, which is notorious for its lack of network reception. He sighed and continued driving towards Meander.

Meanwhile, unbeknownst to Zafar, danger lurked nearby. Just a few hundred kilometres away, militants had seized his brother, shrouding the road ahead in a veil of perilous uncertainty.

# 11

# The Eid Burial

At a relatively secluded stretch on the Nowgam–Pulwama Road, the militants ordered the driver to stop the car. Three of them dragged a semi-conscious Aurangzeb out of the vehicle, while the fourth aimed the muzzle at the driver and asked him to flee for his life. In the whole abduction, the cab driver escaped without a bruise, which in itself appeared too ideal to be genuine.

It was as if entering a parallel universe, where one side was adorned with scenes of domestic bliss—Ammi was standing at the rustic earthen stove, her silhouette bathed in the warm glow of flickering flames. Each gentle stir of the sheer korma vessel was a labour of love. Her weathered hands moved with a rhythmic grace as her face beamed with a peaceful smile, anticipating the moment she would hug her warriors. The aroma of saffron and cardamom weaved through the air like an invisible tapestry, wrapping the room in a cocoon of nostalgia and anticipation. Salani was getting bejewelled like a new bride, a kaleidoscope of colours wrapping it like a comfort blanket, prepping for the impending Eid celebrations. Meanwhile, Aurangzeb's siblings gathered like a constellation of stars, their laughter and chatter filling the room with excitement and camaraderie. They sat close, hearts filled with anticipation as they dreamt of the moments they would share with their beloved brothers, Qasim and Aurangzeb. While carrying out the customary tidying of the house and the area around it, they ended up splitting into two teams with a bet in place—out of Qasim and Aurangzeb, who would be getting their Eid outfits that year? With toys and sweets to be lost in the bet, they waited with baited breaths to welcome their brothers. Every corner of the house came alive in no time and bore witness to their preparations, from the meticulously arranged cotton mattresses to the freshly swept floors.

Meanwhile, in a world far removed from the warmth and safety of their home, Aurangzeb's reality was a harsh and unforgiving one. Bound by a thick jute rope, tightened around his ankle, Aurangzeb was dragged across the rugged terrain, his body bruised and battered by the relentless march of time and circumstance. At every curve, the jagged stones would tear at his flesh, leaving angry welts all over his body that would prick with every pull.

Even though Aurangzeb's vision blurred, first because of the jolt of the gun, then by the haze of pain and exhaustion caused by each collision, a flicker of determination burnt within him—a stubborn refusal to surrender to despair.

Getting dragged away from everything he knew, recognized and loved, he clung to the memory of his family, their faces a beacon of hope in the darkness that surrounded him. And though the unforgiving journey seemed long and unpredictable, he refused to lose hope. Even in the depths of despair, Aurangzeb remained a fighter—a solitary figure getting dragged through the thicket, but with his courage undeterred. He felt lifeless but would constantly shake his head as a reminder to himself that he had to live for his country, for his family.

Aurangzeb's painful journey came to a close, and as he gained consciousness, he found himself tied from his waist to the trunk of a tree, his limbs stretched to their limits, rendering him utterly defenceless.

'*PoK phone lagao. Huzur ko ittalla karna hai*' (Call PoK. We need to inform our sir), one of the terrorists spoke while tightening the noose around the tree trunk. Another militant splashed a bucket full of water on Aurangzeb's face to bring him back to consciousness. '*Uth jaa. Sasural aa gaya hai!*' (Wake up. We have reached your in-laws' place), one of them smirked.

When Aurangzeb looked up, he didn't have an iota of fear in his eyes. Even though he knew that this might be the end of the road for him, he had to ensure that the honour of the Indian Army was upheld.

'*Bhaijaan, PoK call nahi lag raha. Kuch network issue hai*' (Brother, I can't connect with anyone in PoK. It seems like a network issue), the terrorist standing at a distance spoke while swinging the device in the air. '*Koshish karte raho*' (Keep trying), the so-called leader of the pack replied. '*Bhaijaan, iss kafir ka ek video bana lete hain. Social media pe daal denge. Hindustan bhi toh apne sipahi ki halat dekhe ki humse bhidne ka natija kya hota hai*' (Brother, let's make a video of this infidel. We will post it on social media. India should also see the condition of its soldier and what is the result of fighting us). As the red dot on the phone screen was pressed, the militant started interrogating Aurangzeb:

Militant: *Kya naam hai tera?*
(What is your name?)

Aurangzeb: *Mera naam—Aurangzeb.*
(My name is Aurangzeb.)

Militant: *Baap ka kya naam hai?*
(What is your father's name?)

Aurangzeb: *Mohammad Hanief hai Abu ka naam.*
(My father's name is Mohammad Hanief.)

Militant: *Kidhar ka rehne wala hai?*
(You belong to which place?)

Aurangzeb: *Poonch.*

Militant: *Duty kidhar hai?*
(Which is your place of duty?)

Aurangzeb: *Shadimarg Camp, Pulwama.*
Militant: *Kya duty hai teri?*
(What is your duty?)

Aurangzeb: *Main sipahi hoon. Ek tarah se jo post pe duty deta hai.*
(I am a soldier. I am stationed at the post for surveillance and security.)

Militant: *Mehmood bhai aur Tallah bhai ke encounter mein tu he tha?*
(Were you part of the encounter of Mehmood bhai and Tallah Rashid bhai?)

Aurangzeb: *Haan, main he tha.*
   (Yes, I was there.)

Militant: *Tallah logon ka encounter tune kiya hai?*
   (Did you kill Tallah and his comrades?)

Aurangzeb: *Haan.*
   (Yes.)

Though the video was circulated across various social media platforms, the terrorists failed. Contrary to their wish, the camera didn't capture a petrified soldier but a brave tiger, a man whose eyes brimmed with pride as he answered all the questions without fumbling a single syllable. That day, Aurangzeb proved that he was a real fighter, a brave son of a veteran soldier.

The sun was right over the head, and with no contact across the border, the militants started feeling jittery. Finding a new way to kill time, they began employing methods designed to inflict both physical agony and psychological torment on Aurangzeb. One of the militants approached Aurangzeb and pressed a searing cigarette against his flesh. Each burning sensation left behind a painful mark, but failed to get a reaction out of Aurangzeb. The militants used other instruments of torture just as viciously to break Aurangzeb's spirit. The methods of the militants were ruthless and unforgiving, designed to break the soldier's spirit and extract information through sheer terror.

Yet, amidst the searing pain and overwhelming fear, the soldier remained resolute. Though his body bore the scars of their brutality, Aurangzeb's spirit remained unbroken, fuelled by an inner strength and defiance that refused to be extinguished. Through gritted teeth and clenched fists, he endured each torturous action and with each passing moment, his resolve hardened. Though his body may have been broken, his spirit remained unyielding—evidence of the indomitable will of a true warrior.

'Mercy' was a word the militants had never heard of. They kept burning parts of Aurangzeb's body and pulled out six of his nails while blood oozed from the wounds. Even after being constantly tortured for over an hour, the militants couldn't extract anything more than his name and place of duty, a few facts that they weren't oblivious to. When Aurangzeb didn't prove to be of much help, their desperation skyrocketed. One of them immediately pulled out a knife from his pocket. Aurangzeb looked up and tried to break free from the clutches, but there wasn't much he could do being tied to the sturdy tree. '*Abhi bhi mauka hai. Humare saath aaja, teri jaan bach jayegi*' (You still have a chance. Join us in our mission and your life would be spared), the ruthless terrorist said, wiping the knife on his trouser. '*Tujhe kya lagta hai tu zinda hai? Saans lene ko zinda hona nahin bolte. Kuch paison ke liye apna zameer bech chuka hai tu, meri kya jaan bakshe ga?*' (What do you think, you're alive? Breathing is not considered being alive. Your conscience is already dead. For a meagre amount, you have sold yourself. Who are you to spare my life?), Aurangzeb smirked, clenching his jaw while his body was writhing in pain.

Enraged, the militant charged at Aurangzeb, partially slitting his throat. As soon as the knife pierced through his tender flesh, Aurangzeb screamed: '*Abu!*' (Father), a scream so shrill and loud that it could shake one to their very core. All the militants clapped mid-air and laughed. '*Ab dheere dheere marte hue soch tune kya bola'* (Now die a slow death and think about what you said), the militant fumed.

Aurangzeb looked towards the sky. The left side of his neck was bleeding, with ten fingers and four nails, and his body painted with burn marks—he was helpless. This was the price he was paying for loyalty, for his unflinching commitment to protect the honour of India. What was his fault? Was it that he eliminated a few nefarious elements who had taken innocent lives? Or was it that it was his childhood dream to don the olive-green uniform?

On 14 June 2018, Aurangzeb was paying the price for our freedom. He was getting tortured so that we could be safe in our homes.

A few hours had passed, and Aurangzeb was hanging by a thread, thanking the almighty for every next breath as he lay in a puddle of blood. By then, in order to save himself, the cab driver had gone to the nearby police station to report the incident. The local SHO immediately informed the 44 Rashtriya Rifles Unit Headquarters. In a matter of minutes, the unit was ready to launch the operation. The Company Commander gathered the troops in a huddle as the loud war cry—*Bajrangbali ki jai*—echoed through the hills of Kashmir. The unit split into teams and started the search operation in different directions. This operation was unlike any other as it was more personal. One of their own was abducted, and God alone knew what all he had to endure. Every soldier of the company had anger painted on their face as they rushed to find their buddy as soon as possible.

Back home in Salani, the family, oblivious to Aurangzeb's ordeal, was all set to welcome the two soldiers. Qasim arrived first with Zafar, and the house lit up like a carnival. Ammi kissed his forehead as he touched his parents' feet and hugged them, the warmth of which he had been craving for months. The younger siblings were particularly excited as they ran from one room to another with happy chatter all around. Shehnaaz and Zafar were particularly enthusiastic as Qasim Bhai had not bought the Eid outfits, which meant that they had won the bet. They were anticipating Aurangzeb's arrival with bags of goodies any moment now.

A few houses away, the scene was similar. Ilham was busy prepping for Eid. It was a very special one as both Ilham and Aurangzeb had decided to inform their parents about their fondness for each other this time around. As she lay in bed, appreciating her sun-yellow zardozi suit, she imagined herself in Aurangzeb's arms—the man in a white Pathani suit (complimenting outfits was Ilham's forte), and his beloved in a beautifully hand-embroidered salwar kameez. '*Ya Allah! Maine toh Aurangzeb ko apne suit ka colour bataya he nahi. Ab voh matching chudiyan kaise layega Poonch se?* (Oh God! I didn't inform Aurangzeb about the colour of my outfit. How on earth will he get matching bangles for me from Poonch?), Ilham sighed, hitting her head with a pillow. Little did she know that while she was dreaming of a life together with her soldier, he was fighting for his life, unsure of witnessing another sunrise.

Ammi's eyes were fixated on the village approach road when the phone rang. It was an unknown number flashing on Mohammad Hanief's phone. In order to not disrupt the merriment, he went to the outer courtyard to receive the call. In a matter of seconds, the phone slipped from his hand and he came crashing down. Hearing the loud thud, the family rushed outside, only to find their father in a state of shock, lying almost lifeless on the mud floor. An officer from 44 Rashtriya Rifles had called to inform that Rifleman Aurangzeb had been abducted by militants near Kalampora Village while he was on his way home. '*Abu, kya hua? Abu?*' (Father, what happened? Father?) Qasim started patting his father's face. Hanief couldn't move a limb or breathe; a black cloud erupted in front of his eyes. Looking at her husband's face, Raj Begum knew something wasn't right. '*Qasim ke Abu, Aurangzeb kahan hai?* (Qasim's father, where is Aurangzeb?), Raj Begum pulled on his collar as tears rolled down her face. Hanief's voice was thick with emotion—'*Unit se phone aaya tha ki Aurangzeb ko atankwadiyon ne agwah kar liya hai, pata nahi kaise*' (Someone from the unit called informing that Aurangzeb has been abducted by militants while he was on his way home. I don't know how), Hanief replied as he held his head between both his hands. Like a sudden clap of thunder on a clear summer day, the mood at Aurangzeb's residence shifted as shock registered on the faces of everyone gathered. Their joy extinguished in an instant as the weight of the news settled upon them like a sudden downpour. The once bustling room was now filled with a profound sense of grief and sorrow. The festive decorations and sumptuous feast were forgotten in the wake of the tragedy. In that fleeting moment, a chilling silence enveloped the room, casting a pall of unease over the family. Sensing the weight of the tension, Shabbir drew upon reserves of inner strength to steady himself, his voice like a beacon of reassurance amidst the palpable fear. '*Jevi bhai*,' he began, his words a defiant declaration against the silence, '*Sher hai humara, use koi hara nahi sakta, jald hi ghar aaenge. Parson Eid bhi toh hai. Aurangzeb bhai ne aaj tak har Eid ghar par he manayi hai*' (Our brother is a tiger, a force to be reckoned with. No adversary can conquer his spirit. He will soon stride through that door. Aurangzeb has never been away from home on Eid). With each word, Shabbir willed courage into existence, as his unwavering faith in his elder brother was like a balm for the anxious hearts around him. The promise of his brother's imminent return infused the air with renewed hope. Word of Aurangzeb's abduction raced through the village like wildfire, spreading alarm and urgency with every whisper. In the blink of an eye, a wave of concern swept over the community, drawing forth a sea of faces etched with determination and resolve. Within moments, the humble abode of Mohammad Hanief became the epicentre of a gathering storm as thousands of villagers converged upon the scene, armed with an array of makeshift weapons hewn from the tools of their trade—rustic implements of farmers, stout sticks and Dao blades—all gleaming with unspoken purpose. In the midst of the throng, a palpable sense of solidarity and determination took root, binding the villagers and family members together in a shared resolve to retrieve Aurangzeb from the clutches of his captors. Anger simmered beneath the surface, transforming the once tranquil faces of the villagers into marks of steely resoluteness. All they wanted was to reach Kashmir and kill those who had dared to abduct their son.

In the thick of the tumult, officers and soldiers arrived from the Krishna Ghati Brigade to support the family in such testing times. Their arrival was a soothing relief for frayed nerves, a reminder that the community was not alone in its hour of need. With their guidance and assistance, the frenzied crowd was gradually brought under control. Their righteous anger was soon tempered by the steady hand of authority. Villagers dashed back and forth; each driven by a fervent desire to elevate the anguish that had befallen Mohammad Hanief's family. In the middle of the frenzied activity, Ilham, startled by the tumultuous clamour, abandoned her duties in the kitchen and hastened to investigate. Her eyes widened in astonishment as she beheld her father retrieving an ancient revolver from a dusty, time-worn trunk tucked away in a corner of the room. The trunk, weathered and worn by the passage of time, bore the scars of countless years of neglect. *'Abu, aap kahan jaa rahe hain? Aur revolver?'* (Father, where are you going? And why do you have a revolver in your hand?) Ilham's voice trembled with concern as she confronted her father, her heart pounding with a mix of fear and confusion. *'Beta, tum yahin ruko. Pata chala hai ki Aurangzeb ko atankwadiyon ne aghwa kar liya hai. Ab hum ghar par thodi baith sakte hain'* (My child, you stay here only. I have learned that militants have abducted Aurangzeb. We can't sit at home upon learning about this), her father replied solemnly. Ilham's heart shattered into a thousand pieces at that moment. The news was like a blow to her chest, knocking the breath from her lungs and leaving her reeling in disbelief. Tears welled in her eyes as she grappled with the enormity of the situation, and her mind became a whirlwind of fear and uncertainty. Every fibre of her being cried out for action, for justice, yet she felt powerless to do anything but watch helplessly as her world crumbled around her; it was like her very soul had been torn apart. Confusion and panic gripped her, leaving her unsure of how to react or where to turn. Amid her turmoil, one thing kept her going—a deep belief that her love was alive. This belief was her anchor, giving her strength. Without a moment's hesitation, Ilham dashed out of her house, her mind focused on one destination—the mosque. In her rush, she didn't even notice she was barefoot and the sharp edges of rocks were piercing her soles. But the pain was nothing compared to the anguish in her heart. Every step she took was driven by a desperate need to find solace in prayer, to connect with the divine, praying for her love.

She reached the mosque breathless and frantic, yet her determination was unwavering. With tears streaming down her cheeks, she hurried to the spot where she had prayed countless times before, each time Aurangzeb embarked on a mission. It was a place imbued with their hopes, dreams and the promise of his safe return. Kneeling down on the cold stone floor, Ilham poured out her heart in prayer. Her words were a fervent plea, a prayer woven with love and desperation, ringing through the quiet walls of the mosque. At that moment, she felt a deep connection to Aurangzeb, as if their love and faith were weaving together to overcome the distance between them. She drew strength from memories of their time together and the promise of their love. The memories flooded her mind—their laughter, their dreams, their promises of a future together—all now threatened by the cruel reality of his abduction. But amidst the despair, a flicker of faith burned brightly within her. She held onto it fiercely, like a lifeline in the stormy sea of uncertainty. Ilham continued to sit there in the mosque, her prayers becoming a whispered plea for Aurangzeb's safe return punctuated only by her silent sobs. Her heart knew he was alive and all she had to do was pass on the strength to Aurangzeb through her prayers. Each word echoed in the stillness of the prayer hall, carried her hopes and fears to the heavens above. The world outside faded away as she found solace in her faith, clinging to the belief that their love would bring him back to her side.

The phone rang. One of the militants rushed, '*Bhaijaan, huzur ka call hai sarhad paar se*' (Brother, the boss is calling from across the border). The leader of the four immediately answered the call and after exchanging courteous pleasantries, kept nodding his head. Though deep in pain, Aurangzeb was aware of what was happening around him. He knew that this call held the power to determine his fate—whether he would live to see another day or succumb to the merciless hands of his captors. The militant on call remained stoic, his expressions unreadable as he looked at Aurangzeb with cold detachment. Each nod of his head felt like a verdict, sealing Aurangzeb's fate with chilling finality.

At that moment, Aurangzeb closed his eyes, seeking comfort in the memories of happier times. He pictured his family—their laughter ringing through the halls of their home, their faces illuminated by the warm glow of love and unity. He had dreams for them—big plans and aspirations that now hung in the balance, threatened by the cruel hand of fate. Tariq and Shabbir, his beloved younger brothers— he had hoped to send them to Canada and give them opportunities he never had. His parents, too, deserved a life of comfort and security in the new home he had worked so hard to provide for them. And Ilham—his heart ached at the thought of her, the life they had dreamed of together slipping through his fingers like grains of sand. Fear gripped his heart as he wondered if he would ever see her again. Images of their time together flooded his mind—their laughter, their dreams, their promises of a future. Would their love have to wait another lifetime? Ilham's face was the last image he wished to see before his eyes closed. Would she be able to forgive him? Did she even know how much he loved her? Aurangzeb wished he had said 'I love you' more often. As these thoughts consumed him, a single tear escaped Aurangzeb's eye, tracing a path down his bruised and battered face. It was a tear of sorrow, of longing, of the unbearable weight of unfulfilled dreams. The uncertainty of his fate meant their love story might have to wait for another lifetime. It pained him deeply to think of Ilham waiting for him, not knowing if he would ever return to her embrace.

And then, in an instant, the call was severed. The silence that followed was deafening, a stark reminder of the hanging sword looming over Aurangzeb. Just then, the leader of the militants, his face a mask of cold indifference, cast a silent command to his subordinates with a single nod, a gesture laden with deadly intent. In that fateful moment, the air cracked with tension as the militants raised their weapons as one, their movements synchronized with chilling precision. The sound of gunfire shattered the stillness of Gusso village, where each shot echoed through the dense thicket like a thunderclap. The militants unleashed a torrent of bullets upon Aurangzeb. Each impact sent shockwaves through his body, a stark reminder of the fragility of life and the brutal reality of the situation. As he struggled against the ropes binding him, the world seemed to blur into a frenzy of smoke and gunfire. Aurangzeb, his body wracked in pain, felt a searing agony as the bullets tore through his flesh, each impact a cruel reminder of his vulnerability. Fifteen bullets tore through his chest, each devastating blow threatening to extinguish the flame of his spirit. Yet, in the middle of the brutality and carnage, Aurangzeb remained defiant, his will to survive unbroken even as his body betrayed him.

In those final moments, as darkness closed around him, Aurangzeb's thoughts turned to his loved ones—his family, friends and beloved Ilham. He felt a surge of sorrow and regret, knowing that he would never have the chance to fulfil the dreams he had held so dear. But in the pain and despair, there was also a flicker of something else—a quiet resolve, the determination to face his fate with dignity and courage. As the world faded into darkness, Aurangzeb's final emotions were a testament to the indomitable strength of the Indian Army soldier—a silent defiance against the cruelty of fate and the brutality of the attackers. The last sight that Aurangzeb witnessed before being one with the fairies was the sunset— though it wasn't the same, the sight meant that he and Ilham were not over. They would meet in some other lifetime and fulfil their dream of a house together, where she would make kahwa and the two would enjoy each other's company with, of course, the setting sun in the backdrop.

There, in that moment, tied to a tree, Aurangzeb breathed his last. As his bloodstained the earth beneath him, his spirit soared free. The perpetrators, with their dark deed done, fled the scene, leaving behind nothing but a blood-soaked soldier with a pierced chest.

The militants may have shattered his body, but they could not crush the unyielding spirit that burned within him. Though they aimed their weapons at him, their barrage of bullets could not pierce the unwavering love he held for his homeland, for India. They may have succeeded in taking his life, but they could never erase the legacy he left behind. His courage, his sacrifice and his persistent devotion would live on. Though his physical form may have been brought to the ground, his legacy would endure, a shining example of what it means to be truly courageous, patriotic, and Indian.

There in that moment, tied to a tree, Aurangzeb breathed his last. A few hours had passed since Aurangzeb's soul had left his body. His unit's soldiers were frantically looking for their buddy with optimism painted on their faces. It was then that a few women from a nearby village wearing phirans and their heads covered walked in Aurangzeb's direction. They were out to collect firewood for their next meal. The moment they saw a man lying lifeless next to the tree, soaked in blood, they cried out for help. On hearing the urgent screams of the women, the village elders rushed to the scene. The man was no more but he was a soldier or so it seemed from his ID card. When they informed the local police station about the incident, the SHO immediately called 44 Rashtriya Rifles and gave them the directions to Aurangzeb's location. The unit rushed to the site but their speed came to a screeching halt when they saw their fellow soldier lying on the ground.

The militants had subjected their friend to brutal torture. Each member of the 44 Rashtriya Rifles was deeply affected, overwhelmed by sorrow and disbelief. The soldiers were like a close-knit family, and seeing one of their own suffer such a tragic fate ignited a fierce anger within them. Some even rushed forward, hoping against hope that he would wake up, shaking him gently and calling his name with desperate voices. Tears welled in their eyes as the reality sank in—their friend and fellow soldier was gone. Anguish swept through the soldiers like a tidal wave, mixed with anger at the injustice of it all.

The Company Commander, usually composed and stoic, knelt beside Aurangzeb. His hands trembled as he reached out, brushing away a lock of hair from the fallen soldier's face. He closed his eyes briefly, trying to hold back the tears that threatened to overwhelm him. Around him, the other soldiers stood in solemn silence, their faces etched with grief. Each person remembered moments shared with their fallen comrade—Aurangzeb, his bravery, his laughter in lighter moments, their shared hardships during missions and the unspoken bond that only soldiers understood. Now, seeing him in such a state, it was incomprehensible. How could someone so strong and resilient be brought down in such a cruel manner?

The journey back to their company base with Aurangzeb's mortal remains was a sombre procession through the rugged landscape that had been their battleground and their home. Each soldier riding in the convoy felt a profound sense of loss. They had lost more than a comrade; they had lost a brother, a friend and a steadfast companion in their shared struggles. The convoy moved slowly, as if reluctant to reach their destination and face the stark reality awaiting them at the company location. The dust kicked up by the convoy settled slowly, like a shroud over their hearts. Every bump in the road felt like a gentle reminder of the hardships they had faced together and the ultimate sacrifice Aurangzeb had made. Finally, they had arrived.

The camp was hushed, the usual bustle replaced by a heavy silence. The Company Commander led the way with a heavy heart, his steps measured yet burdened with the weight of accountability. The soldiers gathered around a simple platform where Aurangzeb's coffin lay draped in the national flag. The sight struck them like a blow to the chest—it wasn't just Aurangzeb they had lost; it was a part of their own spirit that had been torn away. The view of the Indian Tricolour brought a mixture of pride and sorrow to their hearts— pride for Aurangzeb's service and sacrifice, and sorrow for his untimely departure from their ranks. The wreath-laying ceremony began with solemn reverence. Wreaths were placed beside Aurangzeb's coffin, each one a token of gratitude, love and respect. The soldiers approached one by one, their movements slow and deliberate. Their hands, calloused from years of handling rifles and ropes, trembled as they reached out to touch the flag-draped coffin. Some whispered words of farewell as their voices choked with emotion. Some touched the coffin gently, as if trying to awaken their fallen friend from a deep sleep. Others stood with heads bowed, their hands trembling as they whispered prayers for Aurangzeb's journey to the beyond. Tears ran down their faces, each one revealing the deep emotions stirring within these tough soldiers. The tears that fell were not signs of weakness but of a profound bond that transcended the battlefield. These were men with chests of steel, accustomed to standing firm in the biting cold of Siachen or the scorching heat of Rajasthan without flinching. They were soldiers, yes—brave and disciplined. But beneath the olive-green exterior beat hearts that could ache with profound sorrow. Their hearts were tender beneath the camouflage and medals, capable of feeling pain just as keenly as pride. Aurangzeb wasn't just a fellow soldier; he was their brother-in-arms. His loss cut deep, like a wound that refused to heal.

The Company Commander, usually a pillar of strength, struggled to maintain his composure. His eyes, generally sharp and alert, were now clouded with tears that he did not try to hide. He had lost soldiers before, but Aurangzeb's death struck a chord deep within him. He had watched Aurangzeb grow from a young recruit into a seasoned soldier, admired for his bravery and respected for his loyalty. When he spoke of Aurangzeb's bravery, his loyalty and his unwavering commitment to their mission, he recounted moments of camaraderie and shared hardships, highlighting Aurangzeb's role as a pillar of strength within their unit.

As the ceremony came to an end, a profound silence enveloped the camp. The soldiers stood in a circle around Aurangzeb's coffin, their heads bowed in a final moment of respect and farewell. In that poignant moment, nature seemed to offer its own tribute. Birds sang softly from the branches of nearby trees, their melodies weaving through the quiet air like whispers of condolence. Leaves rustled in the breeze as if the trees themselves were bowing in reverence to the fallen soldier. The soldiers, their faces touched by the soft golden light of dusk, felt a deep connection to the earth beneath their feet and the sky above. The tranquillity of the evening was a stark contrast to the turmoil in their hearts. Each breath they took was heavy with the weight of loss and the bond they shared with Aurangzeb. They had fought together, laughed together and now mourned together.

As the time for Aurangzeb's departure drew close, the soldiers carried with them the memory of Aurangzeb—his laughter, his bravery and the indelible mark he had left on their lives. The setting sun dipped below the horizon, casting a final, fleeting glow over the camp. And though the soldiers walked away with heavy hearts, they knew they would forever carry Aurangzeb's spirit with them, guiding them through the challenges yet to come.

Soon after, the soldiers prepared for the helicopter journey to 92 Base Hospital in Badami Bagh Cantonment, Srinagar. The helicopter awaited them with its blades beating a steady rhythm, like the pulse of their collective sorrow. The cabin was cramped yet comforting, offering a shared space to mourn and reflect. With heads bowed and hearts heavy, the soldiers glanced at each other with eyes that spoke volumes— eyes filled with sorrow, resolve and an unspoken vow to honour Aurangzeb's memory.

The journey was not just a physical transport; it was a spiritual passage through memories and emotions. The helicopter soared over rivers that mirrored the soldiers' unspoken tears, and forests that whispered of battles fought and victories won. Each passing moment seemed to draw them closer to their destination and further into their shared grief. As the helicopter gently touched down on the helipad at Badami Bagh Cantonment, Srinagar, the soldiers disembarked with grave resolve. They formed a tight formation around Aurangzeb's coffin, their steps measured and respectful, and moved with a synchronized grace born of years of training and discipline. Each step forward was deliberate, a silent tribute to the weight they carried—not just the physical weight of the coffin, but the emotional weight of loss and remembrance.

While the entire family in Salani rolled the prayer beads in hope for a positive news, Tariq was away. He had gone to Pune for his military selection test and boarded the next flight to Jammu the moment he received the news of Aurangzeb's abduction.

Back in Salani, the officer who was with Aurangzeb's family informed Hanief that they had found Aurangzeb, his body. At that moment, Hanief felt as if somebody had pulled his soul out of his chest. The officer's words struck Hanief like a lightning bolt. He stood there, stunned and paralysed by the news of Aurangzeb's fate. Without a moment's hesitation, he fled to the fields, desperate to shield his family from the unbearable truth. Hidden among the swaying maize plantation, Hanief crumpled to the ground. He clutched his handkerchief to his mouth, choking blood-curdling screams that tore through his soul. Tears streamed down his wrinkled face. In the stillness of that moment, memories of Aurangzeb flooded Hanief's mind—his stubborn childhood, the pride Hanief felt every time he looked at Aurangzeb and dreams for a future now shattered.

Alone in the fields, he surrendered to his pain, allowing his tears to speak the unspeakable sorrow of a father who had lost his beloved son. The biggest loss for a father is the loss of his young blood, a weight so heavy that Hanief's aging heart couldn't bear. Hanief composed himself for the sake of his emotionally broken family and reached home. Raj Begum, surrounded by the village women, hugged her son's photo while praying for his safety. She didn't know that her son had left on a journey from where there was no return. She didn't know that she would no longer hear the sound of his voice or see his innocent smile. All she wanted was for Aurangzeb to return home. Kilometres away, Aurangzeb was getting ready in Srinagar to embark on his final journey home.

As fate would play out, Tariq's aircraft landed in Srinagar due to some technical snag. As soon as the aircraft descended, he switched on his phone to his father's message: 'Aurangzeb shaheed ho gya'. Sitting alone on the window seat of the aircraft, Tariq felt as if the seats were closing in on him and the sounds of co-passengers were getting distant. Unable to process the news, he immediately rushed towards the cockpit to speak with the captain and somehow managed to disembark at Srinagar airport as the aircraft was heading back to Pune. As he made his way to Badami Bagh Cantonment, he was hoping for it to be a terrible prank. Aurangzeb was his backbone; how would he function now?

But it wasn't a prank. As Tariq moved closer, he saw Aurangzeb's barren body—there were more bullet holes than skin on his chest. His brother had been tortured beyond belief. Being the only one from the family who saw every detail, every cut and every bullet that pierced through his brother, Tariq broke down. Looking at his brother, lying lifeless and tortured to death, he felt furious yet helpless. He wanted to run and slaughter all those who inflicted this pain on his brother but knew that he couldn't. Aurangzeb had been the one holding the family together; how would they survive now?

For Tariq, he was not just a brother but also a father figure and his best friend, to whom he confided his deepest fears and fondest desires. He knew that he had to hold himself together for his parents and siblings. That is the beauty of family—all of them broken yet standing composed for each other. Tariq washed Aurangzeb's body with his own hands and helped wrap him ceremoniously. That night, nobody slept in Salani. While everyone else was sitting in anticipation of hearing some positive tidings about Aurangzeb, Hanief crouched in a corner—he couldn't look Raj Begum in the eye.

The next morning, though it was Eid, gloom had engulfed Mohammad Hanief's home. Somehow, Raj Begum had received the news that Aurangzeb was in Srinagar and was on his way home along with Tariq. She immediately wiped her tears, adjusted her dupatta and rushed to the kitchen to prepare his favourite sheer korma. Her eyes felt heavy but she was relieved her favourite child was coming home. Even the siblings were busy tidying up the house to welcome their brother. Little did they know that though Aurangzeb was coming home, he would not be able to taste ammi's delicacies.

Hanief had gone to speak with the maulvi regarding the cremation and returned home to a rather shocking scene. He rushed to the kitchen to find Raj Begum lost in thought cooking for her son. 'Arey, aap kahan the? Aurangzeb Srinagar mein hai aur jaldi ghar aane wala hai. Dekha, koi bhi Eid Aurangzeb ghar se door nahi manata' (Where were you? Aurangzeb is in Srinagar and he will soon be home. Every year, he is home for Eid and this year is no different). Raj Begum looked excited as she stirred the vessel. Hanief was shocked. He picked up the hot vessel from the stove and threw it on the floor. He couldn't keep the news to himself anymore. It was time his family knew that Aurangzeb was on his way home, but not to celebrate Eid; he was coming to be buried in the land where he was born. Raj Begum couldn't believe what she heard and collapsed, surrounded by her children who couldn't stop crying. Hanief knelt down, sprinkled water on his wife's face and wrapped her in his arms. They may have lost Aurangzeb but they had to be strong for each other. Raj Begum surrendered to Hanief, though the wails of a mother brought the entire village to their home.

Back in Srinagar, after the wreath-laying ceremony, the bullet-laden body of Rifleman Aurangzeb was flown from Badami Bagh Cantonment to Salani for the last rites. While the helicopter descended in Salani, the sound switched. Instead of the familiar whirr of the rotor blades, there was something else—a mother's anguished cry, a raw and heartbreaking lament that blanketed the town of Salani.

As the helicopter gently descended on the ground, the mother's wail reached its peak, a piercing cry that touched the very soul of everyone present. Rifleman Aurangzeb's casket was ceremoniously marched to his family home. Thousands of people had gathered to pay their respects to a warrior. Raj Begum couldn't hold herself and she sat hugging her son's casket, crying incessantly. Shehnaaz, Shabbir and Zafar huddled together remembering their beloved brother. Aurangzeb's youngest siblings Shazia and Asim rushed towards Mohammad Hanief howling. The old man didn't know whom to look towards, whom to hold. He moved towards Raj Begum and told her that the day Aurangzeb had donned the uniform, he was no longer their son. He was India's son and had lost his life while fighting for his motherland.

Aurangzeb died with his boots on, he didn't succumb under the pressure of the brutal forces. Amongst the cries, anger and frustration, one person stood under the khubani tree, broken in silence. Ilham couldn't come to terms with the fact that her journey with Aurangzeb had ended. Since the moment she had seen Aurangzeb's tricolour-wrapped casket, her lungs had not taken a full breath. She couldn't even gather the courage to take a step forward towards Aurangzeb because he wouldn't reciprocate. He wouldn't bring her bangles anymore or catch sunsets with her. She would never be able to embrace his hand again. He had promised to formalize their relationship this Eid, but he had only kept half of it. He came home but for her to meet him one last time. She felt alone in a world full of people, lost in her own village and amongst her people. He was gone, she had to believe, but he lived on, only she knew. Standing amidst known faces, she felt cloistered. Ilham found herself adrift in a sea of memories, clinging to the fragments of a love that had once illuminated her darkest days. Yet, like a flame extinguished by the winds of fate, their love remained but a fleeting ember in the vast expanse of eternity. Ilham's heart, heavy with the weight of grief and longing, yearned for Aurangzeb's presence, the warmth of his embrace and the whispered promises of a future that would never come to pass. And so, in the aftermath, their love remained forever frozen in time.

As preparations began for Aurangzeb's last journey home, a tide of support rose across the country. People from all walks of life, moved by his courage and sacrifice, reached out to honour the fallen soldier.

It was time for the final walk. As the family, with Aurangzeb resting on their shoulder, marched towards the burial ground, they felt as if their feet were tied by an iron chain. Every step they took, pulled the life out of them. For a man, the most difficult day is when he has to carry the weight of his son on his shoulders. Mohammad Hanief carried Aurangzeb to his grave. People came in thousands as they witnessed the gun salute given to a brave soldier. Thrice, the sand had to be taken out from Aurangzeb's grave as the number of people kept multiplying. This is what Aurangzeb had earned—respect. A person's real value is seen not in how many people come to celebrate with him but in how many people come to bid him final goodbye. In death, Aurangzeb had become more than a soldier. He had become a symbol of courage, loyalty and the indomitable spirit of a nation.

That tragic day, it poured in Salani. It was as if the clouds shattered and the earth was in mourning as the nation lost its brave son. Aurangzeb did return home for Eid, but he didn't wear the Pathani suit or have his ammi's sheer korma. The nation may have moved on, but Mohammad Hanief's family has not celebrated Eid since 2018.

* * *

Years have passed since that fateful summer day when Rifleman Aurangzeb made the ultimate sacrifice for his nation. The world has moved on, new conflicts have arisen and other heroes have emerged. But in the quiet village of Salani, and in the hearts of those who knew him, Aurangzeb's memory burns bright. The family now lives with one aim—avenging the death of their beloved son and brother, Rifleman Aurangzeb.

Mohammad Hanief's household, once lit up with laughter and dreams, today, stands silent honouring the courage of their son. Mohammad Hanief, his back a little more bent with age, enjoys his afternoon siesta under the same khubani tree that saw all of Aurangzeb's tantrums unfold. Even today, he is a pillar of strength. Whenever someone speaks to him about Aurangzeb, he starts with 'my son', his eyes light up and his voice becomes thick with emotion.

Raj Begum, her hair streaked grey now, doesn't get tired of telling tales of her beloved son. She has since stopped making sheer korma. She realized that her nightmare from years ago had come true—God had shown her Aurangzeb's end while she was still carrying him.

Qasim and Rubeena were blessed with a baby boy called Ayaan a year after their marriage. Aurangzeb would fondly call him Ayaan Tiger. Every single day, when the sun shifts west and the stars twinkle, Ayaan rushes out to say hello to his dear *chacha*.

Along with Qasim, Shabbir and Tariq have also joined the Indian Army to take their brother's legacy forward. Their sole aim is to avenge Aurangzeb's death and march on his path to safeguard the nation. Now, the tradition in the family has changed. The brothers no longer visit the masjid first on every leave. Instead, before going home, they visit their beloved brother resting in Salani. Aurangzeb's grave has become their masjid and mazar.

Ilham lives with memories—memories of her love, laughter and Aurangzeb. People often tell her that life continues after someone dies, and she agrees. For her, it's possible to survive but impossible to truly live without Aurangzeb. She can smile but not laugh; she can cry but not shed a tear; she has things to say, but he won't be there to listen. Deep down, she still hopes that, just as the earth revolves, Aurangzeb might find his way back to her. Until another lifetime, their love will continue to exist.

As she sat on the wooden bench next to the river, Ilham looked up—a beautiful sunset, wasn't it?

\* \* \*

*The story of Rifleman Aurangzeb became a rallying cry, a reminder of the cost of freedom and the valour of those who defend it. For his selfless service, devotion to duty and indomitable courage in the face of the enemy, Rifleman Aurangzeb was awarded the prestigious Shaurya Chakra posthumously by the Honourable President of India Smt. Droupadi Murmu in 2023. The award was ceremoniously received by his parents—Mohammad Hanief and Raj Begum.*

\* \* \*

# Acknowledgements

Well, here we are! The book is finished (finally). Writing this book has been a journey—sometimes, it felt like a marathon and other times, like I was trying to sprint up a mountain in flip-flops. But here we are, and it's only fitting that I take a moment to thank those who made this possible.

To my readers—thank you. Yes, *you*. For picking up this book, for giving it a chance and for reading my words without running away screaming. You've made this process all the more worthwhile, and I hope you find something in these pages that resonates with you. If nothing else, I hope I entertained you. And if not, I'll buy you a coffee and we can chat about why.

To the family of Rifleman Aurangzeb—thank you for your unwavering courage and for sharing your story with me. You are the true heroes, and I am just lucky to have been able to tell a fraction of your story. You gave me the privilege of capturing your son's legacy, and I will forever be in awe of your strength and grace. *This book is as much yours as it is mine.*

To my parents—thank you, thank you, thank you. You've been the backbone of this book, not just with your love and encouragement but with your *unbelievable* patience. For all those hours I cocooned myself in the corner of my room, on the floor with my laptop, barely emerging for food or air, you didn't just let me be—you *understood*. You didn't ask me a million questions about what I was doing or why I looked like I hadn't seen sunlight in weeks. Instead, you silently slid a cup of coffee under the door (because that was the only way I'd notice it) and let me get back to writing. You believed in me when I didn't believe in myself. And when I'd surface from my writing cave, half-dazed and sleep-deprived, you were there with a listening ear, a hug or just some quiet support. You gave me the time and space I needed to focus, and you were always there to pick me up when I stumbled. This book wouldn't exist without your love, patience and the countless cups of coffee you brought me without my asking. You're my forever inspiration. I love you more than I could ever say.

To Manish—thank you for being the commissioning editor I didn't know I needed. You didn't just edit this book; you shaped it, moulded it and helped it find its soul. Your feedback was always thoughtful, insightful, and—when necessary—exactly the tough love I needed.

To Radhika and Rachna—thank you for handling the book contract with such grace and professionalism. You made sure everything ran smoothly behind the scenes, allowing me to focus on the writing while you took care of the legal details like a pro.

To Aparna—thank you for being my lifeline during the editing process. Your support as the copy editor went above and beyond, and you were always available on WhatsApp (even at weird hours, sorry about that!) to discuss every tiny detail. You read through the book multiple times, tirelessly fixing inconsistencies and making sure it was polished to perfection. Your meticulous attention to detail made the book so much stronger, and I can't imagine having gone through this process without you by my side.

To my special someone—Well, where do I even start? You've been my partner through this whole journey, and not just in the *writing* part (though your support with that was amazing). From the first draft to the final edit, you've been my sounding board, my therapist and my greatest source of encouragement. You believed in me when I didn't believe in myself, gave me pep talks when I wanted to quit and made me laugh when I thought I was going to lose it. Through every doubt, every moment of panic, you were there with just the right words (and sometimes, just a comforting hug). You're the reason this book exists, and I can't thank you enough for your love and patience, and for just being *you*. Every word of this book carries a little bit of you in it. You truly are my rock. Thank you for making this whole journey so much easier— and for not running away when I started talking about plot points at 2 a.m. G, I love you 3000.

And to everyone else who played a role, big or small— thank you. Your support, whether it was a simple 'good luck' text or a more hands-on role in this process, has meant more to me than you'll ever know. This book wouldn't be what it is without each and every one of you.

So here it is, my heartfelt thank you to everyone who's been part of this adventure. Your love, support and belief in me have been the fuel that kept this project going. I am forever grateful. And now, I'm off to celebrate with a cup of coffee and possibly another rewrite (just kidding . . . or am I?).

Scan QR code to access the
Penguin Random House India website

On the fateful day when the news of Tallah Rashid's demise hushed through the mansion, Masood Azhar was ensconced in his private study—a bastion within the mansion where he conducted all his strategic affairs and received updates from his network of operatives spread across the valley.

He sat at an enormous mahogany desk, its surface scattered with maps, correspondence from sympathizers and a metal brass lamp that cast a warm yellow glow across his weathered face. Panelled with dark wood, the walls were lined with shelves that sagged under the weight of leather-bound volumes nestled alongside stacks of handwritten notes. On one wall behind his expansive desk, hung a large map of the Kashmir valley, meticulously marked with coloured pins and annotations. Each pin denoted a significant location—a strategic stronghold in the valley, a sympathetic village, military installations, routes of ingress and egress or a potential target. The map was evidence of Masood Azhar's attention to detail and his strategic mind, which constantly plotted and reevaluated the chessboard of destruction. It was not just a geographical representation but a canvas upon which Masood Azhar stretched his dreams of destabilizing India's hold over the region of Kashmir. Alongside the maps, sketches and diagrams adorned the wall, depicting various scenarios of insurgency and resistance. These were not just theoretical musings but practical blueprints born from years of covert operations and intelligence gathering. Detailed plans for infiltrating border crossings, disrupting communication networks, and inciting local unrest were meticulously laid out in intricate details, which showed Masood Azhar's grasp over asymmetrical warfare. What Masood Azhar failed to notice was that India as a country is not so fragile that it can be broken by some self-proclaimed godman sitting across the fence, but of course, a man could dream. As he received the news of Tallah Rashid's demise, the room seemed to contract around him, enclosing him in a bubble of solemnity. His brows furrowed momentarily, showing a rare glimpse of vulnerability beneath the mask of stoicism that he often wore. He slowly rose from his chair, his hands gripping the edge of the desk as if to steady himself against the weight of the news. The silence in the room was palpable, broken only by the distant sounds of the mansion's guards patrolling the grounds outside. In that sombre moment, Masood Azhar made a decision. His voice, typically grim and measured, now resonated with a steely determination as he recorded an audio message for his followers and supporters.[39] His words carried both mourning for the fallen and a call to rise against those they perceived as their enemies.

*Mere bhanje Tallah Rashid ki maut bekar nahi jayegi. Jannat mein usse ucch sthan milega. Shaheed ke marne ka inkaar nahi, voh zaroor mara hai, lekin unke murda hone ka inkar hai. Voh maut aane ke baad bhi murda nahi hua. Inhe murda kahoge toh Quran ke nafarmaan, inhe murda samjhoge toh Quran ke nafarmaan. Toh phir hum inhe kya samjhein? Voh zinda hai, inhe zinda maano, inhe zinda samjho. Haan unki yeh zindagi tumhari mehdood akal se samjhi nahi jaa sakti, magar tumne na arsh dekha hain na kursi par yakeen rakhna zaroori hai ki arsh bhi hai aur kursi*

[39] 'Masood Azhar releases an audio clip after his nephew Talha Rasheed killed in an encounter', IndiaTV, 10 November 2017, https://www.youtube.com/watch?v=Nhyb8uEsYqw.

*bhi . . . Aur issi tarah yeh yakeen rakhna lazmi hai ki shaheed zinda hai.*

*Deewane ko salaam!*
*Shaheed ke liye allah taala ke pass 5 inam hain: -*

1) **Khoon ke pehle katre ke saath jannat mein uska makaam dikha diya jata hai**
2) **Usse Azaad -e- Kabr se bacha liya jata hai**
3) **Qayamat ke din ke badi ghabrahat se voh mehfooz rehta hai**
4) **Uske sarr par Waqar ka Taaj rakha jata hai, jo duniya ki tamaan cheezon se behtar hai**
5) **72 hoorein jinse uska nikaah kar diya jayega**

*Tum uss nafarmaan shaks ko le aao, jinhone mere bhanjhe, humare doston ko jannat pahunchaya hai.*

**Sab kuch luta ke. Rah-e-mohabbat mein ahale dil,**
**Khush hain ki jaise Daulat-e-Konain paa gaye,**
**Shahne chaman ko apni baharon pe naaz tha,**
**voh aa gaye,**
**Toh saari baharon pe chaa gaye**

The death of my nephew Tallah Rashid will not go in vain. He will attain a high place in Paradise. There is no denial of a martyr's death; indeed, he has surely died. But to deny them the status of a martyr after his death is to disobey the Quran. If you call them dead, it is disobedience to the Quran. If you consider them dead, it is disobedience to the Quran. So then, how should we understand them?

They are alive, believe them to be alive, consider them alive. Yes, your limited intellect cannot comprehend this life of theirs, but just as you believe in the Throne without having seen it, it is necessary to believe that both the Throne and the Chair exist... And similarly, it is essential to believe that the Martyr is alive.

Salutations to the passionate one!

For a martyr, Allah has 5 special rewards:

1. **Before the first drop of blood, his place in Paradise is shown to him**
2. **He is saved from the terror of the grave**
3. **On the Day of Judgment, he remains safe from great fear**
4. **A crown of honour is placed on his head, which is better than all the worldly treasures**
5. **He will marry 72 beautiful companions (hoors)**

Bring that disobedient person here who has led my nephew and our friends to Paradise.

*Having sacrificed everything in the path of love,*
*The people of the heart are so happy,*
*As if they have gained the wealth of the entire universe.*
*The king of the garden took pride in his own springs,*
*But when they arrived, they spread over all the springs.*

The audio file, carefully scripted and recorded in a secure location, served as a rallying cry to indoctrinate and mobilize the youth, who were seen as vital recruits in his fight for the so-called liberation of Kashmir. In it, Masood Azhar vividly

# #5

# Death of Humanity

## 1 November 2017

Tallah Rashid and his group of militants, accompanied by Wasim Ahmad Ganie, started their descent from the upper reaches of the steep snow-clad mountains. They moved on foot under the moonlit sky and marched like dark shadows through the dense wilderness of the valley. After travelling for a few days, they finally reached Aglar Kandi village in Pulwama district, where they had to stay put for the following two days. A huge ammunition consignment was to be picked up from the village to aid them in achieving the goal they had set out to accomplish.

Meanwhile, at Shadimarg Camp location, Aurangzeb and his company soldiers were braving frequent skirmishes with the stone pelters now and then. They were also getting a lot of intel about the movement of militants from time to time. Still, the biggest intel reached them on 7 November when they were informed that a group of militants under the command of some foreign terrorist, apparently an A++

category militant,[37] had reached Aglar Kandi village late last night. The informer also told them about some consignment the militants had been waiting for, and his expectation that they were surely planning something big. With the help of disguises, the militants merged with the local population of the village so as not to get caught. This was a valuable piece of information. The company commander of 44 Rashtriya Rifles gathered his troops. After delineating their roles, the soldiers huddled as the echo of their war cry—'*Bajrang Bali ki Jai*' (Hail God Hanuman) resounded through the mountains of the valley. They then left for Aglar Kandi village without wasting a crucial minute.

## 7 November 2017

The crisp winter morning in Aglar Kandi village began like any other, with smoke curling from chimneys and villagers going about their daily routines despite the underlying daily tensions in the valley. The aroma of freshly baked bread travelled through the narrow lanes as children walked their way to school and women in groups moved to collect firewood. Unbeknownst to the villagers, Tallah Rashid and his men had arrived under the cover of darkness, their presence cloaked in

---

[37] The militants are segregated into various categories – A, A+, A++, B and C by the Police. A+ and A++ represent the highest threat levels, including top commanders and those involved in major attacks. A Category encompasses militants who have been active for a considerable time. B Category comprises militants with a moderate level of involvement in operations but they do not hold leadership positions. C Category typically includes newly recruited militants or those with minimal involvement in militant activities.

secrecy as they awaited the arrival of a crucial consignment. Dressed in winterized fatigues that obscured their identities, they seamlessly blended into the fabric of the rural landscape. As the sun rose higher in the sky, the group visited the village masjid to meet someone and collect information regarding the anticipated conquest. Just then, a local sympathizer loyal to the cause of Kashmiri independence hurried through the narrow alleys and whispered urgently into Tallah's ear—the Indian military had received intelligence of their presence and an outer cordon was already in place as the soldiers were swiftly mobilizing towards the village.

As Tallah Rashid received the urgent warning about the approaching military operation, a surge of adrenaline shot through him, instantly sharpening his senses. The gravity of the situation weighed heavily on his shoulders—the success of their mission, the safety of his men and the looming threat of capture or worse. In that tense moment, a cascade of thoughts raced through Tallah's mind. He knew the stakes were high— any misstep could jeopardize their current operation and the broader struggle for Kashmiri independence, to which he had dedicated his life. His pulse quickened, but outwardly, he maintained a calm and collected demeanour—a testament to years of training and experience in the face of adversity. Tallah's immediate reaction was one of swift decisiveness. He rapidly assessed their options, knowing that time was of the essence. He knew that escape wasn't an option at that moment because of the tightening cordon and they had to take cover. With the sympathizers' information fresh in his mind, Tallah immediately relayed orders to his men, directing them to disperse and seek cover. It was a calculated move to evade the tightening net of the military cordon and maintain an element of surprise—a critical advantage in their asymmetrical warfare against a well-equipped adversary.

While others split into small groups, dispersing into the serpentine network roads in the village, Tallah and Wasim dashed towards the village's modest clinic. The village clinic in Aglar Kandi was an unassuming structure nestled amidst ancient walnut trees, its whitewashed walls weathered by years of harsh winters and scorching sunlight. A faded sign above the entrance of the clinic bore the words: 'Primary Health Centre'. The caduceus symbol on the signboard was obscured by layers of dust and neglect. Inside, the clinic exuded a sense of peaceful sanctity, indeed an ironic place for Tallah to seek shelter. The waiting area of the clinic, which was sparsely furnished with wooden benches worn down by generations of villagers, greeted its visitors with a faint scent of antiseptic blended with the earthy aroma of medicinal herbs. Sunlight filtered through narrow windows, casting dappled patterns on the tiled floors, where patients awaited their turn with quiet resignation.

In one corner sat an elderly man, his weathered face etched with the lines of wisdom and hardship. He cradled a gnarled walking stick in his hands, his gaze distant yet filled with quiet resolve. Beside him, a child no older than five fidgeted intermittently, her small frame wrapped in a shawl knitted with intricate patterns sitting on her mother's lap. Opposite them, a pregnant woman reclined on a makeshift cot, her swollen belly protruding beneath her turquoise sozni-embroidered phiran. She rubbed her belly gently, murmuring soothing words to the life growing within her—a fragile